A History of TCM

*The Thomas Cooper Memorial Church,
Lincoln (c. 1695–2015)*

To Barnabus & Tabea
Every blessing in Jesus
as you serve Him together
Clive 23/4/23

This book is dedicated to Colin Wood
(25.2.1936 – 15.4.2014)
a dear friend and brother in Christ,
member and Deacon of
Thomas Cooper Memorial Church, Lincoln

A History of TCM

The Thomas Cooper Memorial Church,
Lincoln (c. 1695–2015)

Compiled and edited by
Clive E. M. Birks

Published by:
CRB Associates
9 Church Lane
Potterhanworth
Lincoln LN4 2DP
E: info@crbtypesetting.co.uk
W: www.crbtypesetting.co.uk

First published 2015

The photographs on pages 77, 102, 108 (top), 110, 111 and 114 (bottom) are used by kind permission of Lincolnshire Archives.

The photographs on pages 91, 108 (bottom) and 109 are copyright © *Lincolnshire Echo*. Used by permission.

The photographs on page 148 are reproduced by kind permission of Day One Publications.

ISBN 978-0-9932375-0-8

Typeset by CRB Associates, Potterhanworth, Lincolnshire
Printed in the United Kingdom

Contact details:
The editor, Clive Birks:
E: crbclive@fastmail.co.uk

TCM Baptist Church:
High Street, Lincoln LN5 7RN
T: 01522 526149
E: admin@tcmlincoln.co.uk
W: www.tcmlincoln.co.uk

Contents

Acknowledgments 7

In appreciation 8

Editor's preface 9

Introduction 13

1. A brief historical overview 15

2. In the beginning . . . 51

3. The growth of the church and buildings 56

4. Rebuilding the church 63

5. Thomas Cooper Memorial Church (Part 1) 72

6. Thomas Cooper Memorial Church (Part 2) 84

7. Thomas Cooper Memorial Church (Part 3) 92

Appendix 1: Thomas Cooper 134

Appendix 2: Cecil H. Radford 137

Appendix 3: TCM Preachers and Pastors 142

Appendix 4: Miscellaneous 144

Bibliography 160

Acknowledgments

I gratefully acknowledge the assistance of many people and organisations without whom the compilation and publication of this book would not have been possible. In particular, my thanks are due to the following:

The Wood family, for giving permission to access Colin's files and for their help and contributions to the text.

Steve and Jacqui Holman, Eric and Linda Oxby, and other long-standing members of TCM for supplying details and photographs of events which occurred during their lifetime.

The Elders and Deacons of TCM, who have granted me unrestricted access to archived documents held by the church, and to Chris Booth, who has located and supplied them.

Lincoln Central Library, Lincolnshire Archives and the *Lincolnshire Echo* for granting permission to reproduce various photographs from their archives.

The Angus Library, Regent's Park College, Oxford, and Amsterdam City Archives, for access to archived material.

My long-suffering wife, who has endured boxes and documents being strewn around our home for many months, and for her patience while I've spent hours on end reading material and at my computer.

Jesus Christ, and a church where He is Lord!

Clive Birks

In appreciation

When Colin began his research into the history of TCM – and way before then – he had no idea that his original idea would turn into the tremendous document it is now. My family and I can never show our appreciation and thank Clive enough for what he has done, for the hours of research and work he has done to compile this wonderful little book.

After many hours of research and typing, Colin's computer crashed and he lost all he had done apart from his notes. Unfortunately, his illness made it difficult to carry on, and it lay on his desk only just started. Clive took up the baton, managed to retrieve what had been lost on Colin's computer, and went back even further in time to produce a most comprehensive, accurate and fascinating account of the Baptist movement in this county and TCM's part in it.

I know Colin would have been thrilled and deeply humbled at what Clive has achieved. We trust and pray that you will be blessed as you read it, and be thankful to God that the gospel continues to be faithfully proclaimed at TCM.

To God be the glory

Ruth Wood

Editor's preface

This work was in the process of being prepared by Colin Wood when his computer hard drive 'crashed' and none of the files could be accessed. Prior to his death in April 2014, local attempts to recover the data had proved unsuccessful and the work remained incomplete. The Wood family graciously gave me permission to use a professional company in a further attempt to recover the files, with a view to finishing the work begun by Colin as a legacy, and a tribute to a dear brother in Christ. Data recovery was successful, and the family provided a number of documents from which Colin had been working.

One of these documents was *The History of the General Baptist Church in Lincoln now known as the Thomas Cooper Memorial Baptist Church*[1] by W. S. Linton (1911), the then Church Secretary, which was Colin's starting point. The text begins with the following words:

> Before we can fully appreciate the significance of the history of the Thomas Cooper Memorial Baptist Church, it is necessary to know a little of the background to the origins of the Baptist denomination in England, and also something about those who suffered and endured persecution and exile . . .

1 The TCM Library and a number of TCM members have various copies of this document, and an original copy is held by the Angus Library, Regent's Park College, Oxford.

Reading these words made me realise how little I knew about the background to the origins of the Baptist denomination or of the suffering and persecution involved. My interest in this period had also been aroused following presentations on local connections with the Pilgrim Fathers given by Sue Allan, the 'Mayflower Maid' at New Horizons[2] meetings at TCM. A tour – the 'Mayflower Trail'[3], run by Sue Allan – of a number of locations in the area where those who became known as the Pilgrim Fathers met, added further to my interest. In order to further this interest, many hours were spent trawling the internet and referring to a number of books, which resulted in Chapter 1 – 'A brief historical overview: the period culminating in the Protestant Reformation and leading to the emergence of Puritanism and Separatism'. If, like me, your knowledge of this part of history is limited, I hope you will find its inclusion of help in understanding something about those who suffered and endured persecution and exile in order that they might worship God according to their consciences, so that we might have the freedom to worship as we do today.

The following chapters and appendices are the result of delving into old TCM documents, internet searches, valuable contributions from current and former TCM members, and research at the following institutions: Lincoln Central Library, Lincolnshire Archives, Amsterdam City Archives (Stadsarchief Amsterdam), and the Angus Library, Regent's Park College, Oxford.

While every effort has been made to keep this history of TCM authentic, there may well be some inaccuracies in dates

---

2 At the time of writing, New Horizons is a monthly open meeting at TCM providing opportunities for fellowship and sharing the gospel in a friendly environment through an interesting programme, including speakers and organised visits to a variety of venues.

3 For further details visit www.mayflowermaid.com

and certain accounts, as well as missing details. Although republishing of the text in book form is unlikely, notification of any errors or omissions found while reading the text would be appreciated, in order that an electronic version may be updated for future reference. In order to do so, or supply any additional material you may consider should be included, please use the contact details on page 4.

My prayer is, first, that this small volume will be a testimony to the faithful witness of TCM over the years to proclaim the gospel locally, nationally and overseas through its members, and to encourage current and future members of TCM to maintain this uncompromising witness. Secondly, that it provides at least some answers to those enquiring about the history of TCM and asking the question, 'Who was Thomas Cooper?' Finally, that it fulfils my initial intention of providing a fitting tribute to Colin Wood, who, as a member of TCM for so many years, served his Lord and Saviour so faithfully.

Clive Birks
Potterhanworth, Lincoln
May 2015

Introduction

As Baptists, we believe that Scripture teaches plainly and unmistakably that, on profession of faith, we should be baptised (usually by immersion), following the example of Jesus Christ, who Himself was baptised (Matthew 3:13–17; Mark 1:9–11; Luke 3:21–22; John 1:31–34), and instructed His disciples to 'go and make disciples of all nations, baptising them in the name of the Father and of the Son and of the Holy Spirit, and teaching them to obey everything I have commanded you' (Matthew 28:19–20). This was the teaching in the Early Church (Acts 2:38) and its practice (see, for example, Acts 8:12; 9:18; 10:47–48; 16:15, 33; 18:8; 19:5; 22:16).

In this ancient city of Lincoln we have reason to be proud of the fact that we were in the forefront of the great movement which culminated in religious liberty, and also that John Smyth, who historians regard as one of the cofounders of the Baptist denomination,[1] lived and worked in Lincoln and the surrounding area for many years.

Chapter 1 provides a brief historical overview of the period culminating in the Protestant Reformation, the rise of Puritanism and Separatism, including events and the leading figures

---

1 After working alongside John Smyth in Gainsborough and Amsterdam, Thomas Helwys returned to London in the face of persecution and established the first Baptist church in the Spitalfields area of the east end of London during 1611 and 1612 (see p. 47).

involved in Europe and England, particularly those in the area around Lincoln.

Chapter 2 provides information about the early Baptists in Lincoln (c. 1626) and the establishment of the first known church.

Chapters 3 – 6 provide details of the history of the Thomas Cooper Memorial Baptist Church, Lincoln (TCM), from its formation until 1924.

Chapter 7 covers significant work, witness, changes and events since 1924 to the present day (2015).

Appendix 1 supplies some background to Thomas Cooper – shoemaker, poet, Chartist, author, self-taught schoolmaster, journalist and preacher.

Appendix 2 provides some background and a tribute to Cecil H. Radford, Honorary Pastor of TCM from 1924–1958 – thirty-five years of ministry.

Appendix 3 lists all those who from the early days have had the responsibility of preaching, leading or pastoring at TCM, and the dates that they served.

Appendix 4 contains miscellaneous articles and photographs.

Chapter 1

A brief historical overview

The period culminating in the Protestant Reformation and leading to the emergence of Puritanism and Separatism

Although outside the scope of this book, a brief look at Church history shows that errors and superstition were prevalent in the Church even in its infancy. For example, John's letters and some of the other New Testament epistles address early forms of Gnosticism.[1]

Throughout medieval times in England and mainland Europe, the Church was governed from Rome under the authority of the Pope and all church services were conducted in Latin. Most people were unable to speak Latin, and so could not understand the Bible directly. The Church therefore acted as the mediator between God and the people, with priests interpreting the Bible on behalf of their congregations.

Furthermore, at the Council of Toulouse (1229), Roman Catholic church leaders ruled:

We prohibit laymen possessing copies of the Old and New Testament . . . We forbid them most severely to have the above

---

1 A simple definition of Gnosticism is any form of religious belief that emphasises dualism and/or the possession of secret knowledge.

books in the popular vernacular . . . The lords of the districts shall carefully seek out the heretics in dwellings, hovels, and forests, and even their underground retreats shall be entirely wiped out.

(Pope Gregory IX, Council Tolosanum)

Roman Catholic domination, restrictions on access to the Scriptures and erroneous teaching were all contributory factors which, despite the fear of persecution, led to open opposition to the authority and teaching of the established Church, and ultimately gave rise to the Protestant Reformation.[2]

John Wycliffe – 'Morning star of the Reformation'

In the fourteenth century a theologian, John Wycliffe (1320–1384), was an early proponent of reform in the Roman Catholic Church and is considered to be the main precursor of the Protestant Reformation. While studying for his MA at Oxford University he became master of Balliol College in 1360 before gaining his degree and being ordained the following year. Subsequently, he resigned this post and became the absentee rector of Fillingham church, a few miles north of Lincoln, until 1368.

Wycliffe opposed the teaching of the organised Church, which he believed to be contrary to the Bible. In 1378 he wrote *The Truth of Holy Scripture*, breaking with Catholic tradition by declaring the Bible as the ultimate standard by which the Church, tradition, councils and even the Pope must be tested. In his view, Scripture contained everything necessary for salvation; there was no need for additional traditions.

---

2 In simple terms, the splitting of Christianity into Catholic and Protestant Churches.

Furthermore, he advocated that all Christians, not just the clergy, should be able to read the Bible for themselves. With the help of his followers, called the Lollards, and his assistant Purvey, Wycliffe initiated the first translation of the Bible (now known as the Wycliffe Bible) into the English language from the Latin Vulgate, which was the only source text available to him, and in the 1380s produced dozens of hand-written English language Bible manuscripts.

Wycliffe was well-known throughout Europe for his opposition to the teaching of the established Church. Some of his pupils at Oxford were from Bohemia, and took his ideas and copies of his writings home with them, where they influenced the reformer Jan Hus.[3]

Because of his views, in 1381 Wycliffe was banished from Oxford and moved to Lutterworth (near Leicester) where he continued his writings until his death, following several strokes, on 31 December, 1384.

In 1401, King Henry IV enacted a statute making such 'heresy' a secular crime punishable by burning,[4] and in 1408 a convocation in Oxford instituted and enforced a penalty of burning for owning or even reading these translations of Scripture. A Roman Catholic papal decree in 1413 banned Wycliffe's books, and finally in 1415 the Council of Constance

---

3 Among other issues, Hus opposed transubstantiation and the practice promoted by Pope John XXII of selling indulgences (later addressed by Martin Luther). As a result, he was excommunicated, put on trial in 1415 and burned as a heretic.

4 The *De heretico comburendo* was a law passed by Parliament under King Henry IV of England in 1401, punishing heretics with burning at the stake. This law was one of the strictest religious censorship statutes ever enacted in England. The statute declared there were '. . . divers false and perverse people of a certain new sect . . . they make and write books, they do wickedly instruct and inform people . . . and commit subversion of the said catholic faith.' The sect alluded to is the Lollards, followers of John Wycliffe.

ordered his books to be burned and his bones to be dug-up, crushed, burned and scattered in the river – this was carried out in 1428!

However, despite these laws and the severe penalities for breaking them, the Lollards continued to preach.

Some important events in Europe and England

The Gutenberg press – availability of Scripture
In about 1450 Johannes Gutenberg, a goldsmith by profession, developed a movable-type printing press by adapting existing technologies and making inventions of his own. Known as the Gutenberg press, it was capable of producing 3,600 pages per day, and enabled the first mass production of books.

In 1453, Constantinople (Istanbul) was captured by the Turks, resulting in many Greek scholars moving to western Europe with their manuscripts. Translations and printed versions of the Scriptures soon began to appear and be distributed: for example, the Latin Gutenberg Bible (1456), the first Greek Lexicon (1480) and the first printed Hebrew Bible (1488).

A few years later, in 1492, Ferdinand and Isabella expelled around 300,000 Jews from Spain who became exiles all over Europe. With their knowledge of Hebrew and the Hebraic culture, many of them became teachers.

Other publications soon followed: for example, the first Hebrew lexicon (1506); Erasmus' Greek New Testament (1516); the Complutensian Polyglot Bible with Hebrew, Greek and Latin in parallel columns (1517).

These events resulted in an increased knowledge of the Hebrew and Greek Scriptures and a large number of Bibles translated into vernacular languages appearing in England and throughout Europe.

Martin Luther

Martin Luther was born on November 10, 1483, in Eisleben, southeast Germany. In 1498, he enrolled in a school, where he studied grammar, rhetoric and logic – he later compared this experience to purgatory and hell.

In order to train as a lawyer, in 1501 Luther entered the University of Erfurt, where he received an MA degree in grammar, logic, rhetoric and metaphysics. However, in July 1505, Luther had a life-changing experience that set him on a new course. Caught in a horrific thunderstorm and fearing for his life, he cried out to St Anne (the patron saint of miners), 'Save me, St Anne, and I'll become a monk!' The storm subsided and he was saved. Also driven by fears of hell and God's wrath, he became a monk thinking that life in a monastery would help him find salvation.

Luther did not find the spiritual enlightenment he was seeking, and at the age of 27 he had the opportunity to be a delegate to a church conference in Rome. He came away more disillusioned and discouraged by the immorality and corruption he witnessed there among the Catholic priests. On his return to Germany, he enrolled in the University of Wittenberg in an attempt to deal with his spiritual turmoil. He excelled in his studies, receiving a doctorate, and becoming a professor of theology at the university.

While studying Scripture to prepare for a lecture on Paul's Epistle to the Romans, he read, 'The just will live by faith' (Romans 1:17). After meditating on this statement for some time, he realised that the key to spiritual salvation was not to fear God or be enslaved by religious dogma but to believe that faith alone would bring salvation. This period marked a major change in his life and following events gave renewed impetus to the Reformation.

In 1517, Pope Leo X announced a new round of indulgences

to help build St Peter's Basilica. This so angered Luther that on 31 October, 1517, he nailed a sheet of paper containing ninety-five theses to the university's chapel door, intending them to be discussion points, and also sent a copy to Archbishop Albert Albrecht of Mainz, calling on him to end their sale. His *Ninety-Five Theses* laid out a devastating critique of the indulgences and how they corrupted people's faith. The availability of the printing press, allowed copies of the *Ninety-Five Theses* to be distributed throughout Germany within two weeks and the rest of Europe within two months.

In October 1518, Luther was ordered to recant his *Ninety-Five Theses* by the authority of the Pope, but refused to do so unless Scripture proved him wrong. Instead, he went further, by publicly declaring that he didn't consider the papacy had the authority to interpret Scripture, which was a direct attack on the authority of the papacy. In 1520, the Pope issued an ultimatum threatening Luther with excommunication, which Luther burned in public.

In January 1521, Luther was officially excommunicated from the Roman Catholic Church, and in March, he was summoned before the Diet of Worms, a general assembly of secular authorities. Luther refused to recant his statements, demanding he be shown any scripture that would refute his position – there was none. On 8 May, 1521, the council released the Edict of Worms, banning Luther's writings and declaring him a 'convicted heretic', making him a condemned and wanted man. Friends helped him hide out at Wartburg Castle, and in seclusion there, he translated the New Testament into the German language, to give ordinary people the opportunity to read God's Word.

Although still under threat of arrest, Luther returned to Wittenberg Castle Church in Eisenach, in May 1522, where he was able to avoid capture and began organising a new church

– the Lutheran Church. With support from German princes, he gained many followers and Lutherism spread quickly throughout Europe, including Scandinavia.

In 1525, he married Katharina von Bora, a former nun who had abandoned the convent and taken refuge in Wittenberg, and over the next few years they had six children. From 1533 until his death in 1546, Luther served as the dean of theology at University of Wittenberg.

William Tyndale

William Tyndale was born around 1494 in Gloucestershire and educated at Oxford and Cambridge University. Around the early 1520s, Cambridge University was rife with Lutheran ideas. Groups of students were meeting regularly at a secret house called 'The White Horse Inn' to discuss his writings, so it's quite possible that Tyndale became familiar with, and a strong supporter of, the doctrines of the Reformation while studying there. He was ordained as a priest around 1521 and returned to Gloucestershire to serve as a chaplain to a member of the local gentry. During this time, Tyndale's controversial opinions began to attract the attention of the Church authorities.

In 1523, Tyndale moved to London with the intention of translating the New Testament into English from Erasmus' Greek text, an act that was strictly forbidden. He passionately believed that the Bible should determine the practice and doctrine of the Church and that people should be able to read the Bible in their own language. In response to a critic, he is reported to have remarked:

> If God spare my life, ere many years pass, I will cause a boy that driveth the plough in England to know more of the Scriptures than thou doest.

By undertaking this translation, Tyndale was setting himself against the established Church in England, as these ideas were closely associated with Martin Luther and other controversial Protestant religious reformers. In 1524, with the aid of London merchants, Tyndale left England for Germany, where he hoped to continue his translation work in greater safety, and sought out the help of Martin Luther at Wittenberg. Just one year after his English New Testament was completed and printed in Cologne in 1525, friends were smuggling copies into England in cases of merchandise – the first ever Bibles written in the English vernacular. Bishops did all they could to eradicate them, buying them up and burning them – some at St Paul's.

Tyndale's work was denounced by authorities of the Roman Catholic Church and Tyndale himself was accused of heresy. He went into hiding and began work on a translation of the Old Testament directly from Hebrew into English. Henry VIII's break with the Catholic Church in 1534 signalled the beginning of the English Reformation (see p. 25), and Tyndale believed it was safe to carry on his work in public. He moved to Antwerp, one of the main printing centres in Europe, and began to live more openly.

Soon afterwards, Tyndale was betrayed by a fellow Englishman, Henry Phillips. While out walking, he was ambushed in a narrow passage and arrested for heresy by the imperial authorities. He was taken to the state prison in the castle of Vilvoorde, near Brussels, and after more than a year of imprisonment, Tyndale was tried and convicted of heresy and treason. After refusing to recant, he was strangled and burnt at the stake in Brussels on 6 October, 1536. It was reported that before his death Tyndale's last words were, 'Lord, open the king of England's eyes.'

By this time several thousand copies of his New Testament had been printed. Just three years later in 1539, Henry VIII published *The Great Bible* in English based on Tyndale's work. Even though Tyndale's translation of the Old Testament remained unfinished at his death, his work formed the basis of all subsequent English translations of the Bible, including the King James Version of 1611.

John Calvin

John Calvin was born on 10 July, 1509, in Noyon, Picardy, France. As a student in Paris, he studied the liberal arts before studying theology. Later, he pursued an education in civil law in Orléans and graduated as a Doctor of Law, before returning to Paris in 1531.

During his time in Paris, Calvin left Roman Catholicism and joined the Protestant movement, subsequently becoming an informal leader to other Paris Protestants. In the preface to his *Commentary on the Psalms* he wrote:

> To this pursuit I endeavored faithfully to apply myself in obedience to the will of my father; but God, by the secret guidance of his providence, at length gave a different direction to my course. And first, since I was too obstinately devoted to the superstitions of Popery to be easily extricated from so profound an abyss of mire, God by a sudden conversion subdued and brought my mind to a teachable frame, which was more hardened in such matters than might have been expected from one at my early period of life.
> (John Calvin, *Commentary on the Psalms*)

On reaching Geneva while travelling to Basel in 1536, reformer William Farel persuaded Calvin to stay and help the cause of the church, which he did for two years until anti-Protestant authorities forced him to leave in 1538. He was invited back again in 1541, and upon his return from Germany, where he had been living, he became an important spiritual and political leader. Calvin used Protestant principles to establish a religious government; and in 1555, he was given absolute supremacy as leader in Geneva.

John Calvin was a prolific writer of theology. His most notable work was the *Institutes of the Christian Religion*, the first edition of which was published in 1536 in Latin and intended to be a catechism for French Protestants. It was a short work consisting of six chapters dealing with the law, the Apostles' Creed, the Lord's Prayer, the sacraments, false sacraments, and Christian liberty. After several revisions, the final edition was published in 1559 and differed radically from the original 1536 edition, as it was no longer merely a manual for new believers. Instead, it had grown into a thorough systematic theology comprising four volumes, and dealt with more doctrines of the Christian faith.

Calvin's teaching emphasised the sovereignty of Scripture and divine predestination, a doctrine holding that God chooses who is saved – the elect – regardless of their good works or their faith. He allowed no art other than music, and even that could not involve instruments. Calvin believed that the Church should not be subject to the state, or vice versa. While both Church and state are subject to God's law, they both have their own God-ordained spheres of influence. He repudiated the distinction between 'sacred' and 'secular' duty and the prevailing thought that work is a necessary evil. Rather, he taught that work is a calling from God and, therefore, one glorifies God by working diligently and joyfully. His ecclesiology (the study of the Church) sowed the seeds of modern secular democracy. Calvin did not invent capitalism, but he did teach that one of the rewards of hard work is wealth. His philosophy of work allowed capitalism to flourish where it was practised.

Under his rule, Geneva became the centre of Protestantism, and sent out pastors to the rest of Europe, greatly influencing Presbyterianism in Scotland, the Puritan Movement in England and the Reformed Church in the Netherlands.

Calvin died on 27 May, 1564, in Geneva, Switzerland. It is unknown where he is buried. Today, Calvin remains widely credited as the most important figure in the Protestant Reformation.

Anabaptists and Mennonites

The sixteenth-century Protestant Reformation in Europe produced a number of radical reform groups, among them the Anabaptists. Since many of them had been baptised as infants, they denied the merit of infant baptism and chose to be rebaptised as believing adults. Hence, they were known as *Anabaptists* (Greek: *ana* = 'again'), and regarded the Bible as their only rule for faith and life. Some Anabaptists were revolutionaries; others, such as Menno Simons, were more moderate. Because of their radical beliefs, the Anabaptists were persecuted by other Protestants as well as by Roman Catholics and scattered throughout Europe.

In 1536, Menno Simons (1496–1561), a Dutch priest, gathered the scattered Anabaptists of Northern Europe into congregations. These groups came to be called *Mennonites* and by the late sixteenth century had found political toleration in the Netherlands, particularly in Amsterdam and Leiden.

The Monarchy and Reformation in England

While the Protestant Reformation in mainland Europe was mainly the direct result of opposition to the doctrine and practices of the Roman Catholic Church, the Reformation in England was largely due to the actions of the monarchy and

Church leaders breaking away from the authority of the Pope and the Roman Catholic Church, and the resulting changes in government policy.

Immediately before the break with Rome, the Pope and general councils of the Church decided doctrine. Church law was governed by the code of canon law (laws and regulations made by Church leadership) with final jurisdiction in Rome. Church taxes were paid straight to Rome, and the Pope had the final say over the appointment of bishops.

The progress of the Reformation in England was largely determined by the religious beliefs of the reigning monarchs during the sixteenth and seventeenth centuries. Some of the significant events that took place and those involved during the reign of each monarch are summarised below. Although Lutheran ideas and teaching were being widely discussed by those attending institutions such as Oxford and Cambridge, Tyndale's Bibles were in circulation, and Lollardy and other Protestant voices were still in evidence up and down the country, it was the actions taken by Henry VIII that are generally regarded as formally initiating and giving impetus to the Reformation in England.

Henry VIII (1509–1547)

Henry VIII ascended the English throne in 1509 at the age of seventeen. Before the reign of his father, Henry VII, England had been beset by civil warfare over rival claims to the English Crown. Wanting to avoid similar problems in the future, in June 1509, just before his coronation, Henry VIII received papal dispensation to marry Catherine of Aragon, the widow of his brother Arthur, hoping to provide a male successor. However, despite giving birth to several children, the only one to survive was female (subsequently to become Queen Mary – known as 'Bloody Mary').

During his marriage to Catherine, Henry VIII was an observant Catholic and influenced by his advisors, in particular, Cardinal Thomas Wolsey and Thomas More. In 1521, he wrote *The Defence of the Seven Sacraments* (probably with help from others), defending the Catholic Church from Martin Luther's accusations of heresy, and received the title 'Fidei Defensor' (Defender of the Faith) from Pope Leo X. Wolsey, who became Lord Chancellor, and More, his successor, both persecuted those opposing the doctrines and practices of the Catholic Church, accusing them of heresy. Luther's books and Tyndale's Bibles were seized and burned, and those caught reading them punished. More, in particular, had them imprisoned and many burned at the stake for heresy.

Unsurprisingly, Wolsey had enemies at court, including those who had been influenced by Lutheran ideas, among whom was the attractive and charismatic Anne Boleyn, who had arrived at court in 1522, following her education in France. She was a woman of 'charm, style and wit, with will and savagery' and caught Henry's eye!

As Catherine had been his late brother's wife, towards the end of the 1520s Henry claimed that his lack of a male heir was due to his marriage being 'blighted in the eyes of God' and wanted his marriage to Catherine annulled. On the basis of Leviticus 20:21,[5] Henry asked Wolsey to use his influence in Rome to get a papal annulment of his marriage so that he could marry Anne Boleyn. Wolsey was unable to accomplish this, which resulted in his fall from grace and his indictment in 1529 for praemunire (asserting papal authority above that of the Crown). He died in November 1530 on his way to London to answer a charge of high treason.

---

5 If a man marries his brother's wife, it is an act of impurity; he has dishonoured his brother. They will be childless.

Henry was now exposed to the opposing influences of the supporters of Catherine and the papacy, and those who had been influenced by Lutheran teaching, favouring reform and an end of allegience to Rome. Among these were Thomas More, now Lord Chancellor, and Thomas Cromwell, a Protestant lawyer and a powerful Member of Parliament who had become an advisor to Henry following Wolsey's demise. More initially supported the opinion of the theologians at Oxford and Cambridge that the marriage of Henry to Catherine had been unlawful, but as a staunch Roman Catholic, he refused to accept denial of papal authority. Cromwell, however, saw how Parliament could be used to advance Henry's supremacy in the Church, and to further the Protestant beliefs and practices he and his friends, including Anne, wanted. One of Cromwell's closest friends was Thomas Cranmer, soon to be Archbishop of Canterbury.

The anulment of Henry's marriage to Catherine appeared to be deadlocked until Thomas Cranmer suggested a legal approach. Together with others, in 1530 he compiled the *Collectanea satis copiosa* (a collection of historical documents, including Anglo-Saxon laws) designed to prove that kings of England, historically, had no superiors on earth (including the Pope). Although this meant that the Pope's ruling was illegal, there was a proviso: Henry's marriage could be annulled only with the agreement of the Archbishop of Canterbury. But the then Archbishop, William Warham, didn't agree! Henry's response was to charge all the clergy with praemunire, and after much wrangling the Submission of the Clergy was subscribed in 1532, whereby the clergy gave up their power to formulate Church laws without the king's licence and assent.

By now, Anne was pregnant and Henry needed to marry her for the child to be legitimate. In the event, Archbishop Warham had recently died, and Henry appointed Thomas

Cranmer as Archbishop of Canterbury. Cranmer granted the annulment of Henry's marriage to Catherine, and also pronounced that his marriage to Catherine was against the law of God. Anne gave birth to a daughter, Elizabeth, in September 1533. In response, the Pope excommunicated both Henry and Cranmer from the Roman Catholic Church.

The Break with Rome – Acts of Parliament

The stage was now set for the formal break with Rome, and in 1534 the first Act of Supremacy made Henry VIII the 'supreme head in earth of the Church of England'. Further acts were also passed: the Act of First Fruits and Tenths transferred the taxes on ecclesiastical income from the Pope to the Crown; the Treasons Act, made denial of royal supremacy high treason, punishable by death. Because of his refusal to deny papal authority, Thomas More was executed under this legislation in 1535. In 1536, Parliament passed the Act against the Pope's Authority, which removed Rome's power in England to decide disputes over Scripture.

Although now free of Rome, by the end of 1534, the English Church was still essentially Roman Catholic and its religious doctrine and practices remained unaltered. However, under the influence of Cromwell and Cranmer, things were about to change during the rest of Henry's reign and in the following years.

Dissolution of the Monasteries

In 1534, the Crown was experiencing financial difficulties. Aware that the Church owned between one-fifth and one-third of all the land in England, Cromwell realised that by appropriating it and selling significant amounts to the aristocracy, not only would the resulting revenue resolve the Crown's financial problems, but doing so would also gain the support of the aristocracy for royal supremacy in the event of any future attempts to revert to papal authority.

Cromwell appointed commissioners to visit the monasteries on the pretext of examining their character, but actually to value their assets. The commissioners alleged to have found sexual immorality and financial irregularites in the monasteries, which were used to justify their dissolution.

The dissolutions affected lay people, resulting in mobs attacking those sent to destroy the monastic buildings and revolts in various places in England. One local instance was the Lincolnshire Rising in October 1536, when around 40,000 demonstrators from Horncastle, Louth, Market Rasen, Caistor and other nearby towns marched on Lincoln and occupied Lincoln Cathedral. They demanded the freedom to continue worshipping as Catholics, and protection for the treasures of Lincolnshire churches. The rising began at St James' Church in Louth, and there is a plaque commemorating the occasion opposite the south entrance to the church.[6] It ended shortly afterwards when Henry ordered the occupiers to disperse or face the forces of Charles Brandon, the 1st Duke of Suffolk. Following the rising, two of the main leaders, the vicar of Louth and Captain Cobbler (a shoemaker whose real name was Nicholas Melton), were captured and hanged at Tyburn.[7] A number of the other local ringleaders met the same fate, and Thomas Moygne, a lawyer from Willingham, was hung, drawn and quartered for his involvement.

Immediately following the Lincolnshire Rising a far more serious rebellion began in Yorkshire, known as the Pilgrimage of Grace, which was well led by Robert Aske an able lawyer

---

6 See http://en.wikipedia.org/wiki/Pilgrimage_of_Grace.

7 The Tyburn Tree was the triangular gallows, now adjacent to Hyde Park, where a hundred and five Catholic priests, monks, laymen and laywomen were martyred for refusing to renounce the Roman Catholic Church.

from an important Yorkshire family. After negotiations involving the Duke of Norfolk, the main leaders were arrested, put on trial in London and found guilty of treason. Most were executed in London, although Aske was taken back to Yorkshire where he was executed.

Further rebellions took place in Cornwall in early 1537, and in Walsingham, Norfolk – they received similar treatment.

Cromwell completed the Dissolution of the Monasteries by 1540, sweeping away a huge and privileged clerical society during the process; many of the monks returned to secular life, others were ordered to change their religion and were killed if they refused to do so.

Articles of Faith

Following the break with Rome, the Church of England began examining its doctrinal position in relation to the Roman Catholic Church and the Protestant movements. Prior to Henry VIII's death in 1547, several statements of position were issued, and further amendments were made during the reign of subsequent monarchs.

The first attempt was the Ten Articles in 1536, which incorporated some Protestant thought. These articles referred to only three sacraments – baptism, penance and the Eucharist – rather than the usual seven, which included confirmation, ordination, marriage and the last rites. Thomas Cromwell issued injunctions, taking a moderate stand against images in churches, pilgrimages, and banning some holy days and saints' days.

In 1537, a committee headed by Archbishop Thomas Cranmer published *The Institution of the Christian Man* (also known as *The Bishops' Book*), which together with the Ten Articles incorporated the reforms separating the Church of England from the Roman Catholic Church.

However, although Henry VIII was prepared to accommodate some Protestant thinking into his new Church, he was not comfortable with these changes. From 1539 onwards he reversed most of his previous policies, and introduced the Act of Six Articles which, apart from papal supremacy, returned the Church to orthodox Roman Catholicism. Among other things, transubstantiation and private confession to a priest were reaffirmed, the marriage of clergy was condemned, and vows of chastity were unbreakable. Under this act, heresy again became a felony: Protestants were punished for violating the Six Articles, while papists were punished for denying royal supremacy.

Until Henry VIII's death in 1547, the Act of Six Articles remained the basis of the Church's faith. In 1543, *A Necessary Doctrine and Erudition for Any Christian Man* (also known as *The King's Book*, although only the preface is thought to be by Henry VIII), was published, essentially rewriting *The Institution of a Christian Man*, reintroducing traditional orthodoxy, and simply replacing papal supremacy with royal supremacy. Any traces of Lutheranism were no longer present.

Development and availability of the Bible in English
The Coverdale Bible – Myles Coverdale completed Tyndale's English Bible project, using Luther's Bible and Latin sources to finish translating the remainder of the Old Testament. Known as the Coverdale Bible, it was the first complete Bible in the English language and was printed in 1535.

The Matthew's Bible – Involving no translation, only a compilation of the work of Tyndale and Coverdale, John Rogers (using the pseudonym 'Thomas Matthew') published The Matthew's Bible in 1537. Under the influence of Archbishop Thomas Cranmer, Henry VIII licensed the Bible, and Thomas

Cromwell subsequently encouraged bishops to order copies for their churches.

The Great Bible – In September 1538, Thomas Cromwell issued an injunction requiring every parish to purchase a copy of an English Bible and place it in 'some convenient place' for all to see and read. To meet this requirement, seven editions of the Great Bible (so called because of its size) were printed between April of 1539 and December of 1541, distributed to every church and chained to the pulpit. Authorised by Henry VIII, it was the first English Bible for public use and read aloud in church services – a reader was even provided so that the illiterate could hear the Word of God in plain English.

However, in 1540 Henry began his attack upon the free availability of the Bible, and many parishes were reluctant to use English Bibles on the basis that Bible reading led to heresy. This resulted in many Bibles that had been put in place being removed, and in 1543 the Act for the Advancement of True Religion was passed, restricting Bible reading to clerics, noblemen, the gentry and richer merchants. Women of the gentry and the nobility were only permitted to read the Bible in private – women below gentry rank, servants, apprentices and generally poor people were forbidden to read it at all.

The Succession – Acts of Parliament – Henry's Wives

In order to establish succession to the throne, three Acts of Succession were passed by Parliament during Henry VIII's reign.

The *First Succession Act* was passed in March 1533 (or 1534, depending on the calendar being used). It made Elizabeth, the as yet unborn daughter of Henry VIII by Anne Boleyn, the true successor to the Crown by declaring Mary, Henry's daughter by Catherine of Aragon, to be a bastard. The Act also required all subjects, if commanded to do so, to swear an oath recognising the Act and royal supremacy. Anyone who refused to take the oath was subject to the charge of treason under the Treasons Act of 1534.

In 1536, Henry wished to marry Anne's lady-in-waiting, Jane Seymour. Charges of witchcraft, incest and adultery were brought against Anne Boleyn, resulting in her execution at Tower Green on 19 May 1536. Ten days later Henry married Jane Seymour.

The *Second Succession Act* was passed in June 1536, removing both Mary and Elizabeth from the line of the succession, declaring Elizabeth to be a bastard also, and giving Henry the authority to choose who would succeed him if he died without a legitimate heir, by naming his successor in his last will. As a result, Henry was left without any legitimate child to inherit the throne until Jane Seymour gave birth to his son, Edward, in October 1537. Just two weeks after Edward was born, Jane died on 24 October.

After Jane Seymour's death, Henry VIII remained single until 6 January 1540 when, for political purposes, he married a German, Anne of Cleves. The marriage was declared not to have been consummated and annulled after only a few months on 9 July 1540.

Just a few days later, on 28 July, 1540, Henry married Catherine Howard. Some thirty years younger than Henry, after less than a year of marriage Catherine was seeking the company of handsome young men closer to her own age, and by November 1541 there was enough evidence of her infidelity that Archbishop Cranmer informed Henry of her misconduct. She was arrested for adultery and having betrayed the king, which resulted in her execution on Tower Green on 13 February, 1542.

Henry married his sixth wife, Catherine Parr, on 12 July, 1543. Twice widowed, she was a good wife to Henry, as well as being a loving stepmother to two of his children, Elizabeth and Edward, and personally involved in their education. Catherine was the most intellectual of Henry's wives, with a passionate interest in theology and strong Protestant leanings, which probably influenced Elizabeth and Edward; Mary, considerably older than Elizabeth and Edward, remained strongly Roman Catholic.

The *Third Succession Act*, in which Catherine was influential, was passed in July 1543, and returned both of Henry's daughters, Mary and Elizabeth, to the line of the succession behind their half-brother Edward.

Henry VIII died in 1547, and his nine-year-old son, Edward VI, inherited the throne. Catherine survived Henry and secretly married her old love, Sir Thomas Seymour (Jane Seymour's brother), shortly afterwards. She gave birth to her only child, Mary Seymour, on 30 August 1548, and died only six days later, on 5 September at Sudeley Castle in Gloucestershire.

Edward VI (1547–1553)

As Edward was only nine years old when he became king, he was not much more than a figurehead. Edward's uncle, Edward Seymour, the Duke of Somerset, a Protestant, took power and became Lord Protector. With the support of the young Protestant king, the Duke of Somerset and the Archbishop of Canterbury, Thomas Cranmer, began introducing changes to make England a Protestant state.

In 1547, the Act of Six Articles was repealed in the first Parliament of Edward VI, and injunctions were introduced requiring, among other things, all images in churches to be dismantled. As a result, stained glass windows, shrines and statues were either defaced or destroyed, roods, lofts and screens were cut down, and bells removed. Vestments were prohibited, chalices were melted down or sold, and the requirement of the clergy to be celibate was lifted. Processions were banned, and ashes and palms prohibited. Chantries (endowments for the saying of masses for the dead) were abolished completely.

In 1549, a *Book of Common Prayer*, authorised by an Act of Uniformity, was introduced, followed by a revised, more clearly Protestant, version authorised by a further Act of Uniformity, in 1552. Archbishop Cranmer was the principal author of both versions, and the Acts of Uniformity stated that anyone who attended or administered a service where this liturgy was not used faced six months' imprisonment for a first offence, one year for a second offence, and life for a third.

In the summer of 1549, there were uprisings in the West Country against the Prayer Book, and because of economic and social injustices there was another uprising in Norfolk, known as Kett's Rebellion. The Norfolk rebellion was suppressed by John Dudley, Earl of Warwick, who used his success to bring about the downfall of the Duke of Somerset. John Dudley was now appointed Duke of Northumberland and became Edward's chief advisor, advancing Protestant reform still further. Stone altars were replaced by wooden communion tables, radically changing the appearance and focus of church interiors.

Shortly before his death, Edward VI gave his agreement to Cranmer's 'Forty-Two Articles' in June 1553. These articles were never implemented, due to the king's death and the reunion of the English Church with Rome under Queen Mary I. However, this document, heavily influenced by Calvinist thought, subsequently became the foundation of the 'Thirty-Nine Articles' that were introduced in 1563 during the reign of Elizabeth I.

Aged only fifteen, Edward fell ill in February 1553. When it was realised that his sickness was terminal, the Duke of Northumberland was determined that the religious reforms should not be undone. In an attempt to prevent Mary succeeding Edward under the terms of the the Third Succession Act and England returning to Catholicism and allegience to Rome, a 'Devise for the Succession', was put together in which Edward named his cousin, Lady Jane Grey, as his heir and excluded Mary and Elizabeth. However, when Edward died on 6 July, 1553, this decision was disputed. Within thirteen days Jane was deposed and Mary I came to the throne on 19 July 1553.

Mary I – 'Bloody Mary' (1553–1558)

Shortly after her coronation on 1 October 1553, Parliament met and Mary introduced legislation that proclaimed Henry VIII's marriage to Catherine of Aragon valid and legal. Further legislation abolished the religious laws introduced by Edward VI, restoring church doctrine to that defined in the 1539 Six Articles of Faith, and papal supremacy in England. Mary also abandoned the title of Supreme Head of the Church, and reintroduced Roman Catholic bishops and monastic orders. In November 1554, the Heresy Acts were revived, making it a treasonable offence to believe in a different religion from the sovereign, which carried the death penalty.

Under the Heresy Acts, married priests were deprived of their benefices, many Protestants were imprisoned and 283 were subsequently executed, mostly being burned at the stake. Around 800 chose to go into exile and left the country, including John Foxe, from Boston, who wrote *Actes and Monuments (Foxe's Book of Martyrs)*, an account of Christian martyrs, but highlighting the sufferings of English Protestants during this period.

The Archbishop of Canterbury, Thomas Cranmer, was among those imprisoned and forced to watch while two prominent Protestants, Bishops Ridley and Latimer were burned at the stake. Cranmer briefly recanted, repudiated Protestant theology, and reaffirmed the Catholic faith. Legally, he should have been absolved, but Mary refused to reprieve him. On the day of his burning, in March 1556, Cranmer dramatically withdrew his earlier recantation of the Protestant faith, thrusting his right hand, which he had used to sign his earlier recantation, into the fire first. Reginald Pole was appointed Archbishop of Canterbury immediately after Cranmer's death.

The burnings proved to be very unpopular and generated strong anti-Catholic feeling in England, resulting in Mary becoming known as 'Bloody Mary'. The progress of her intention to return the country to Roman Catholicism was also limited by the vested interests of the aristocracy and gentry who had bought the monastic lands sold off after the Dissolution of the Monasteries, and who refused to return them voluntarily as requested by Mary.

In order to remove her half-sister, Elizabeth, from direct succession and leave a Catholic heir to continue her reforms, Mary married Philip II of Spain in 1554, an unpopular choice and one which produced a protest from Parliament. The marriage was childless, and the alliance with Spain dragged England into a war with France. Discontent grew further when Calais, the last vestige of England's possessions in France, dating from William the Conqueror's time, was captured by the French in 1558.

Following a false pregnancy, Mary became ill and drifted in and out of consciousness. However, at one point she was lucid enough to agree to pass the crown to her half-sister, Elizabeth, and in keeping with the custom Mary's will was read aloud on 16 November. After receiving the last rites, Mary died the next day, 17 November 1558.

At the end of Mary's reign, only a few monasteries and chantries had been reinstated, and Protestants, such as Thomas Bentham, Bishop of Coventry, continued to secretly minister to underground congregations.

Elizabeth I (1558–1603)

As Mary left no heir when she died, her half-sister Elizabeth inherited the throne on 17 November 1558. Together with Edward VI, Elizabeth had been well educated by Catherine Parr and been strongly influenced by Catherine's Protestant teaching, although still retaining elements of Catholic doctrine and practices. Having seen the turmoil resulting from Edward's introduction of Protestant reforms to the Church, as well as Mary's subsequent persecution of Protestants and attempts to restore England to Catholicism, Elizabeth and her advisors sought to establish a Church that embraced most opinions. This resulted in the restoration of the Protestant Church of England through two Acts of Parliament in 1558 known together as the Elizabethan Religious Settlement – the *Act of Supremacy* and the *Act of Uniformity*.

The Act of Supremacy

The Act of Supremacy restored the Acts that Mary had repealed and changed the title of the monarch from 'Head of the Church in England' to 'Supreme Governor of the Church of England', giving Elizabeth ultimate control of the Church. The change may have been made to appease Catholics who could not accept the monarch as 'Head of the Church', or because Elizabeth was a woman. The Act also included an oath of loyalty to the Queen that the clergy and others were expected to take; if they did not do so, they lost their office. All but one of the bishops lost their posts, as did a large number of fellows of Oxford colleges, and many dignitaries resigned rather than take the oath. The bishops who were removed were replaced by appointees who agreed to the reforms.

The Act of Uniformity

The Act of Uniformity established a set form of worship in the Elizabethan Church of England. In 1559 the 1552 *Book of Common Prayer* was reintroduced with a few modifications to make it acceptable to more traditionally-minded worshippers, and was to be used in every church in the England. Church attendance on Sundays and holy days was made compulsory, with a twelve pence fine to be collected if people did not attend (recusancy), the money to be given to the poor. In 1581 an Act was passed increasing fines for recusancy to twenty pounds – an impossible amount for the majority of the population to pay. The Communion wording was deliberately vague so that Protestants and Catholics could both participate, and the ornaments and vestments of the Church were to be kept as they were before the reforms in the second year of Edward's reign. As many in Parliament were still Catholics, there was considerable opposition to the Act, and it was only passed by three votes.

Articles of Faith

Once established, the Elizabethan Church of England began examining its doctrinal position in relation to the Roman Catholic Church and the continental Protestant movements under the direction of Matthew Parker, the then Archbishop of Canterbury. In 1563, the *Thirty-Nine Articles of Religion* were published, defining the position of the Church of England in relation to Calvinist doctrine and Roman Catholic practice.

The articles modified some of the more extreme Calvinist thinking and provided the basis for the unique English reformed doctrine. They were finalised in 1571, and were to have a lasting effect through their incorporation into the *Book of Common Prayer*.

The Geneva Bible, the Bishops' Bible and Archbishops of Canterbury

More and more people were now wanting to read and discover for themselves what the Bible said. First published in its entirety in 1560, the *Geneva Bible* met this need. Its title derived from the fact that it was conceived and printed in Geneva, Switzerland, by a number of Protestant scholars who had fled there to escape from Mary's persecution. It was the first English Bible to use cross-references and use verse numbers for easy reference. In addition, there were extensive notes to help explain and apply the text – in effect the first 'study Bible'.

Because Elizabeth and Church leaders thought the *Geneva Bible* would undermine their authority, as a scholar himself, the Archbishop of Canterbury, Matthew Parker, took on the task of producing an alternative Bible. Portions of the text were assigned to various revisers, the majority of whom were bishops, who, despite their prejudice against it, used the *Geneva Bible* as the basis for the alternative Bible. With the offending material removed, and authorised to be read in church, their work was published in 1568 as the *Bishops' Bible*.

After Matthew Parker's death in 1575 he was succeeded by Edmund Grindal as Archbishop of Canterbury. Grindal had Puritan sympathies, and wanted the Church to be more overtly Protestant. He soon began to make changes, and allowed the publication of the Protestant *Geneva Bible*, which had been suppressed by Parker. This displeased Elizabeth, who did not want the Church to move any further in a Protestant direction. She and Grindal soon clashed over another matter – 'prophesyings', which were unauthorised meetings for prayer and preaching. Elizabeth was concerned that preachers would say whatever came into their head, rather than sound doctrine. She recognised that this could undermine her Church, and also be dangerous, as there was no control over what was said, or the issues that might arise.

In 1576, she ordered Grindal to suppress the prophesyings. However, after consulting with his bishops and finding that the majority approved of them, he refused to do so. He told Elizabeth that although she was the highest authority in the land over political matters, she did not have the same authority over spiritual matters, and that he must put the will of God above his duty to her as sovereign. Elizabeth was outraged at his defiance, and Grindal was suspended from his office in the summer of 1577 until his death in 1583.

John Whitgift, a devoted Anglican, succeeded Grindal as Archbishop of Canterbury. He shared many of Elizabeth's views and aspirations and pushed for obedience to the Elizabethan Church. Whitgift was suspicious of the Puritans, and defended the Elizabethan Church against this group, as well as protecting it against the Catholics.

Events in the Netherlands during Elizabeth's reign

In 1568 a revolt began in the Netherlands against Spanish politics and Roman Catholicism during the reign of Philip II, known as the Eighty Years' War. In 1572 William the Silent (Prince of Orange), invaded the Netherlands with a Protestant army, and during the ensuing struggle with Spain all the northern and a few southern provinces formed an alliance, signing the Union of Utrecht in 1579 and declaring their independence in 1581. Under William the Silent, many persecuted people, such as the Calvinists and Anabaptists, had found asylum and liberty in the Netherlands.

When William the Silent was assassinated in 1584, Queen Elizabeth became aware of the threat then posed by Spain, and provided military assistance to the Dutch. Robert Dudley, Earl of Leicester, was sent to lead the English campaign in support of the Dutch revolt from 1585–1587, and he accepted the post of Governor-General of the Netherlands when it was offered to him. During this time the British Ambassador was William Davison. Assisting Davison in the diplomatic service was William Brewster (see p. 48), which gave him opportunity to hear and see more of reformed religion and develop a real fondness for the Netherlands. When Davison lost the favour of the Queen in 1587 and was dismissed from office, Brewster returned to Scrooby[8] in 1590 to succeed his father as Postmaster.

Effects of the Elizabethan Religious Settlement and the end of Elizabeth's reign
The Elizabethan Religious Settlement resulted in the emergence of several groups, two of which could not be accommodated within the settlement.

The first of these were Catholics who remained loyal to the Pope, and regarded Elizabeth as illegitimate. They had to choose between loyalty either to their Church or their country. Those who chose loyalty to the Roman Catholic Church were regarded as traitors, and for some it meant life on the run or, in some cases, death for treason.

The second group were Protestants who wanted reform to go much further, and who could no longer accept the Church of England as a true Church, believing it to be unbiblical. This gave rise to the formation of small groups of convinced believers outside the Church, known as *Separatists* (see p. 47),

---

8   Scrooby is a small village in Nottinghamshire.

who faced imprisonment and exile as the the government attempted to crush them.

By the time of Elizabeth's death in 1603, within the Church of England itself, there were other groups:

- those wanting to remove any remaining traces of the old ways, known as *Puritans*, who wished to see an end of the *Prayer Book* and episcopacy (the governance of bishops);
- those who were content with the changes introduced by the Elizabethan Settlement – a considerable body of people who were opposed to the Puritans but not loyal to Rome, who rejected prophesyings, who preferred the revised Book of Common Prayer of 1559 (without some of the matters offensive to Catholics), and accepted the governance of bishops.

Although the Church of England was now firmly established, the seeds of future conflict between these groups were already present. This conflict surfaced and became more defined during the reigns of the Stuart kings, James I and Charles I, and the abolition of prayer book and episcopacy by a future Puritan Parliament was one of the factors that contributed to the English Civil War.

Elizabeth died on 24 March 1603 at Richmond Palace. Her coffin was carried downriver at night to Whitehall, on a barge lit with torches. After her funeral on 28 April, the coffin was taken to Westminster Abbey where she was interred in a tomb with her half-sister, Mary.

Only a few hours after Elizabeth's death, James VI of Scotland was proclaimed as James I of England, as she had left no heir.

James 1 of England (1603-1625)

James was the son of Mary Queen of Scots and her second husband Henry Stewart, Lord Darnley. He was a descendant of the Scottish king Robert the Bruce and the English Tudors through his great grandmother Margaret Tudor, sister of Henry VIII. When his mother fled to England, James became King James VI of Scotland in July 1567, at the age of thirteen months. He had various guardians during his early years, and had a thorough education with a heavy emphasis on Presbyterian and Calvinist political doctrine. In 1589 he married Anne of Denmark.

Prior to James moving to London on the death of Elizabeth I to be crowned King James I of England, Archbishop Whitgift had assured James of the loyalty of the Church of England and the bishops. However, on his way to London the Puritans presented to him their 'Millenary Petition' – an unsigned petition expressing the wishes of hundreds of concerned clergymen who wanted to see further reforms in the Church of England and setting out their requirements for amending the liturgy. A three-day conference, with the alleged purpose of discussing these proposals, was held at Hampton Court Palace in January 1604.

As a result of his upbringing and education, James had now come to regard the marginal notes in the Geneva Bible, favoured by the Puritans, as 'seditious, dangerous and traitorous', and detested any form of representative Church government. As king, James believed he had supreme authority and divine right of the crown to govern the Church through the bishops, authorised by the Act of Supremacy and Act of Uniformity. In the event, the conference was significantly biased against the Puritans, who had little opportunity to express their concerns, and were sneered at when they attempted to do so. James terminated the conference and was heard to say about the Puritans, 'I shall make them conform, or I will harry them out of the land, or else do worse.' The conference did produce at least one positive outcome: because of his aversion to the Geneva Bible, James authorised the creation of a new Bible, which resulted in the publication of the King James Version of 1611.

When Archbishop Whitgift died in 1604, Bishop Richard Bancroft was installed as Archbishop of Canterbury. With the backing of James I, Bancroft secured the acceptance by a convocation of the clergy of a new canon law for the Church of England, using the power of his position to institute doctrinal and liturgical standards for priests and bishops – the *Ecclesiastical Constitutions and Canons*, requiring worship to be conducted in complete conformity to *The Book of Common Prayer*. As well as increasing persecution against Puritans and Separatists, Bancroft also increased his attacks on Roman Catholics, determined to root out any vestiges of 'popery' in England. In 1604, around three hundred Puritan ministers were silenced, imprisoned or exiled.

Although failure to conform, or meeting for secret services, was strictly forbidden and regarded as a serious crime, groups of Separatists continued to multiply and flourish. In particular, two closely linked local groups emerged. One group was based in Gainsborough, the other in Scrooby, a small village in Nottinghamshire, not far from Retford. These groups attracted men and women from Lincolnshire, Nottinghamshire and South Yorkshire, some of whom would become the Pilgrim Fathers, emigrating first to Holland and then to America in the *Mayflower* – but that's another story. In tracing the emergence of the Baptist denomination and the establishment of a Baptist church in Lincoln, it is the Gainsborough group of Separatists which is of particular interest.

The Gainsborough Separatists

The Gainsborough Separatists were led by John Smyth. At some point, Thomas Helwys, a country gentleman and lawyer who lived with his wife and family at Broxtowe Hall, Nottingham, developed a close bond with John Smyth, and he and his wife became committed members of Smyth's Separatist congregation. As already mentioned, historians regard John Smyth and Thomas Helwys as co-founders of the Baptist denomination. At this point it's appropriate to include some information about them, not least because of John Smyth's connections with Lincoln.

John Smyth and Thomas Helwys

John Smyth's place and date of birth are unknown, but it is known he trained at Christ's College, Cambridge, where one of his tutors was Francis Johnson, who would lead one of the earliest groups of Separatists to Amsterdam. Smyth graduated with a BA and an MA, and remained as a fellow at Cambridge for a period before being ordained. On the 27 September 1600 he was appointed to the office of Preacher (or Lecturer)[9] to the City of Lincoln with a salary of £40 per year plus £3 6s 8d for house rent and leave to keep three cows on the common. At this time Smyth was a Puritan, faithful to the Church of England. However, he became increasingly critical of the Church of England, questioning whether certain of its practices were based on Scripture and leaning more and more towards Separatist views. As a result, on 13 October 1602 he was released from his duties at a meeting of the Corporation of the City of Lincoln for his 'strange doctrines' and 'forward

---

9 During the sixteenth and seventeenth centuries the term 'lecturer' referred to teachers appointed by Parliament to give instruction in the Christian faith in places where there were few regular ministers.

preaching'. In 1603 he wrote *The Bright Morning Starre* and in 1605 *A Paterne of True Prayer*, criticising the established Church in both of these works.

As many people in the area were attracted to his views, Smyth began holding worship services in Gainsborough in 1602 and became their Pastor. When dissenters were outlawed by James I in 1604, Smyth and his group were allowed to meet in secret in Gainsborough Old Hall by its sympathetic owner Sir William Hickman.

In 1606 Smyth attended an important meeting in the Coventry home of Sir William Bowes with other clergy who had been deprived of their parishes to discuss what course of action they must take. Those present included Richard Clyfton from Babworth and John Robinson from Norwich, who were now leading another group of Separatists (the Scrooby Separatists) meeting in the Manor House in Scrooby, the home of William Brewster, and with whom Smyth's group had a close relationship.

In 1607, the High Court of Ecclesiastical Commission for the Province of York clamped down on the dissenters and because of persecution John Smyth, Thomas Helwys, and a group of church members fled to the relative safety of Amsterdam, to be followed shortly afterwards by a group from the Scrooby Separatists.

For a time they met with the congregation associated with Francis Johnson and Henry Ainsworth, before some differences in doctrine became apparent, especially regarding their understanding of worship and the duties of ministers. In 1608 Smyth outlined these differences in a work entitled *The Differences of the Churches of the Separation*.

Smyth and Helwys shared with other Separatists a desire for a pure Church. On the basis of their reading of Scripture, they insisted that the Church was best organised as a gathered

Chapter 2

In the beginning . . .

The Early Baptists in Lincoln (c. 1626)

The actual date when a Baptist Church was first formed in Lincoln is the subject of speculation. Perhaps some of those returning from Amsterdam with Thomas Helwys came to Lincoln – we don't know. The earliest proof of the existence of such a community in Lincoln is to be found in a letter written in 1626 from five Baptist communities in England, of which Lincoln was one, delivered by two friends commissioned to carry it to Mennonite friends in Holland. The letter deals with points of doctrine, and the opening sentences are as follows:

> To our dear friends, Hans de Ries and Renier Wybrant,
> and their churches, with all the other servants and churches
> walking in the same way with them, and living in Holland
> and in those neighbourhoods; with the churches of Jesus
> Christ, which are in England, and live in London, Lincoln,
> Sarum [Salisbury], Coventry, and Tiverton, all salvation, while
> they heartily wish that much mercy may be multiplied from
> God the Father by our Lord Jesus Christ.[1]

---

1   B. Evans (1864), *The Early English Baptists*, vol. II, p. 26, available in pdf format from the Library of Princeton Theological Seminary, New Jersey, USA.

There is also another letter written in 1630 from the church in Lincoln direct to Mennonite friends in Holland, the opening sentences of which are as follows:

> I acknowledge, beloved and loving friend, that I have received your letter (from the hands of John Drew, our beloved friend,) which was sent to us, and the others of our brethren among this nation; and as we find in it an evidence of your good opinion towards us as regards our Christian condition, we may not neglect to return you our gratitude for it, while we heartily wish that you and we may come to the unity of the Holy Ghost, and to those bonds of peace which are in the truth. Amen . . .
>
> Lincolne, September 5, 1630[2]

The letters are still preserved in the Amsterdam City Archives.[3] At this point, when a Baptist Church is mentioned it refers to a group of people meeting in homes or in the open air; buildings were erected later when numbers became too large to meet in homes.

In 1651 there was a conference of Baptists, probably at Leicester, where thirty churches were represented by two messengers or delegates. The conference drew up a Confession of Faith known as *The Faith and Practise of Thirty Congregations*,[4] and is signed by the two representatives from Lincoln, Valentine James and John Johnjohns.

---

2 B. Evans (1864), *The Early English Baptists*, vol. II, p. 41, available in pdf format from the Library of Princeton Theological Seminary, New Jersey, USA.

3 Archive number 1120/inventory 121: nos. A13758000299 and A13758000300, Amsterdam City Archives (Stadsarchief Amsterdam).

4 The Confession is very rare, copies of the original being found only at the Angus Library, Regent's Park College, Oxford, and at the British Museum.

In March, 1660, the year the monarchy was restored under Charles II, another Baptist conference was held in London at which a further Confession signed by a representative from Lincoln was drawn up, headed as follows:

A BRIEF CONFESSION OR DECLARATION OF FAITH
Set forth by many of us, who are (falsely) called Ana-Baptists, to inform all Men (in these days of scandal and reproach) of our innocent Belief and Practise; for which we are not only resolved to suffer Persecution, to the loss of our Goods, but also Life itself, rather than to decline the same.

Subscribed to by certain Elders, Deacons, and Brethren, met at London, in the first month (called March, 1660.) in the behalf of themselves, and many others unto whom they belong, in London, and in several Counties of this Nation, who are of the same Faith with us.

After the Way which men call Heresie, so Worship we the God of our Fathers; Believing all things which are written in the Law, and in the Prophets, Acts 24,14.[5]

A lengthy Confession based on scriptural quotations follows before the signatures of the representatives. William Paine is one of the signatories, who was a representative of the Lincoln church and later became its minister.

Emerging from the suffering and persecution of the Separatists, these early Baptists, were still to face further trials and hardships. On 19 May 1662, the famous Act of Uniformity was passed. This Act stated that every minister should make a public declaration that he subscribed to all and everything contained in the Book of Common Prayer, otherwise he would be deprived of his living and as far as possible deprived

---

5   http://www.reformedreader.org/ccc/tsc.htm (accessed 30.12.2014).

of obtaining an existence in other occupations. Not content with this, the Ecclesiastical Party passed the Conventical Act, decreeing that any nonconformists attending a conventicle[6] or more than five persons in addition to members of a family assembling together, should be fined £5, or imprisoned for three months for a first offence. For a second offence the punishment would be doubled and for a third offence, it would result in transportation to some 'foreign plantation'. The Baptists of Lincoln, felt these hardships and persecutions, but resolutely remained true to their faith.

Unable to stamp out the defiance of those who would not adhere to these Acts, in 1672, Charles II decided to grant licences as follows:

1. For a particular place to be used for worship other than according to the custom of the 'Established Church'.
2. For a person to teach a congregation in a place named.
3. For a person to teach in any licensed place.

Records of the licences issued are held in The National Archives, Kew, London, and show that licences to preach in Lincoln were granted to two men, namely Roger Fawnes and Nicholas Archer, and the homes of Elizabeth Lylly and John Anderton were licensed for worship.[7]

It is also interesting to note that in Hykeham the home of John Taylor was licensed for preaching, and that there were similar licences granted for places in Bassingham, Carlton-le-Moorland and Stragglethorpe, all near Lincoln, as well as many others throughout the county. In fact, with the exception

---

6   A secret or illegal religious meeting.
7   See also 'The Baptist Licenses of 1672', *Transactions of the Baptist Historical Society*, 1.3 October 1909, pp. 156–177 (esp. p. 158). www.biblicalstudies.org.uk/pdf/tbhs/01-3_156.pdf (accessed 30.12.2014).

of Kent, Lincolnshire was the best provided county for both preachers and preaching places.

Another blow was inflicted in 1673 by means of the Test of Corporation Act.[8] Although this Act was aimed primarily at Roman Catholics, it also fell with equal severity on non-conformists. In February 1685, Charles II died and James II, a Roman Catholic, came to the throne. During his short reign there is no record as to how the Baptists in Lincoln fared. On the 5 November 1688 William of Orange invaded England, and on the 11 December of the same year, James fled to France, leaving England free from the tyranny of the Stuarts.

During the reign of William and Mary things began to improve for dissenters with the introduction of the Toleration Act on 24 May 1689, granting freedom of worship to non-conformists (i.e., dissenting Protestants such as Baptists and Congregationalists). It allowed nonconformists their own places of worship and their own teachers and preachers, subject to acceptance of certain oaths of allegiance. The act did not apply to Roman Catholics and maintained the existing social and political restrictions, including exclusion from political office for dissenters.

It was, however a great step forward, and it seems pretty clear that the passing of the Toleration Act inspired the group of Baptist believers in Lincoln to think of erecting a meeting house for the church, as there is an ancient manuscript in existence, stating that there was a Baptist Chapel in Lincoln in 1695, six years after the Toleration Act.

---

8   The principle was that none but people taking communion in the established Church of England were eligible for public employment.

Chapter 3

The growth of the church and buildings

The first General Baptist Church in the parish of St Benedict (c. 1701 – 1860)

We now begin to reach a period when it can be asserted that a Baptist Church existed in the city of Lincoln, although, if as was stated earlier, there was a building in 1695, its whereabouts is unknown. However, there are documents that give evidence that in 1701, a man by the name of Joseph Veal, presumably a member of the little church, bought a small piece of land in the parish of St Benedict. Two little cottages stood on this land and Joseph Veal, with the assistance of some friends, built a small chapel there and laid out the remaining portion of the land as a burial ground. This was sited to the rear of St Benedict's Square, between the old St Benedict's Church and the River Witham where the river joins the Brayford Pool. The chapel was built behind the cottages and approached via a narrow passage and thus was hidden from public view – a very necessary course to take in those days of persecution.

When Joseph Veal died he left a will dated 26 September, 1703, in which he bequeathed the property to Joseph Isle and others, who held it in trust for the Baptist Church. Keeping the property in private ownership, rather than vesting it to

Trustees, was a safer course, as the property of dissenters was by no means secure. William of Orange had died on 8 March 1702 and had been succeeded by Queen Anne. However tolerant William may have been, Anne was openly hostile to nonconformists. Thus it was a far better course for dissenters to rely upon the honour of each other rather than risk the property being seen as an endowment from a dissenter, but it will be seen later that the intentions of Joseph Veal were honourably carried out when circumstances changed.

In 1703, the church withdrew from the General Assembly of the General Baptists on a point of doctrine, although it is not certain what this was. However, by 1711 there is evidence that the church was back in the Assembly – the Lincoln church had replied to a circular letter from the Assembly, stating that they would do what they could to help defray the charges for ordaining ministers.

We now move on a few years to 1714, when on 1 August of that year Queen Anne died and was succeeded by George I. During his reign the previous hostility towards dissenters considerably weakened and they began to feel more secure.

In 1715, Samuel Elliss was allowed to live in the little cottage in the chapel grounds, and was appointed in return to take care of the meetinghouse. This seems to be the first appointment of a chapel keeper.

In 1726, Joseph Isle carried out the intentions of Joseph Veal when he purchased the property, by transferring it to Trustees for the purpose of a Baptist Chapel. That Trust Deed is the original title by which the church held the property and may still in existence, but untraced to date. The property consisted of a Chapel with a small garret over it and a vestry with a chamber over it, two cottages, the burial ground, and another small cottage at the end of the burial ground.

New Trustees were appointed in 1728 and again in 1740, including William Johnson of Whittlesea and William Penney, both of whom had connections with the Lincolnshire Baptist Association. Other Trustees were Matthew Hursthouse of Spalding, John Wells, Thomas Curtiss and William Ball.

Further changes and appointments of new Trustees were made in 1757 and 1761, one of the new ones being William Thompson of Boston. It appears that in the ensuing years the Chapel began to decline in numbers, and it had not been possible to secure a resident minister. However, the remaining membership held together, and in 1779 Joseph Proud of Fleet was appointed as a new Trustee.

Plaque in memory of William Penney on the rear wall of TCM church

By 1781 the membership had declined to the level at which it was unable to maintain public worship, and the decision was taken to let the premises to the Particular Baptists,[1] with a proviso that General Baptist ministers should be allowed to hold services when they passed that road. Accordingly, a three-point agreement was drawn up with terms as follows:

---

1 The earliest Baptists, led by John Smyth and Thomas Helwys, adopted Arminian views and became known as General Baptists, believing in a general or universal atonement. Later, a group of Calvinists in London, led by John Spilsbury, formed a group which became known as Particular Baptists, who accepted believer's baptism by immersion as the proper form of baptism, but insisted on the classic Calvinistic emphases upon human depravity and of Christ's atonement being limited only to a select group of saints.

1. That the Particular Baptists do enjoy the use of the said Meeting House and burial ground, and garret over the Meeting House, paying the yearly sum of twenty shillings from Ladyday last, to be laid out on the tenements adjoining, until the same are put in tenantable repair, and also that they keep the said Meeting House in good repair at their own proper charge.
2. That any of our Ministers [that is General Baptist] have the liberty to preach in the Meeting House when they travel that way.
3. That the poor woman now in the little room adjoining be permitted to live gratis in the same as usual.

The Particular Baptists apparently used the buildings on these terms for several years until they built one of their own in Mint Street. During these years, the General Baptists and the Particular Baptists appear to have got on well together, except for one occasion, when Mrs George, the poor woman mentioned in the agreement, refused the use of the vestry for their Sunday School and locked the door.

In 1790 a letter was sent to the General Assembly, regarding the Lincoln property and the purchase of an additional cottage. The cottage would be very convenient to use as a passage to the Meeting House as it was near to the River Witham which was used for baptising believers by immersion. The sum of £50 was needed to purchase the property and other churches were asked to assist. By 1793, £30 was still required and five members of the Assembly promised to collect five guineas each to help to complete the purchase. It is not certain whether the full amount was raised, but it would appear not, as the Particular Baptists continued to use the Meeting House under the agreed terms until 1821.

During the years prior to 1821, a new movement had been established among Baptists. Dan Taylor, originally a Methodist from Northowram, near Halifax, had become a Baptist with Arminian views and introduced new ideas and opinions into the denomination which older members refused to tolerate. However, Taylor gathered considerable support and in 1770 this resulted in the formation of the New Connexion of General Baptists.

Moving on to 1803, a man named Mr Vidler of Battle, who had been travelling through Lincolnshire, reported to the General Baptist Assembly, that he had discovered a Meeting House in Lincoln belonging to the Old General Baptists,[2] but was now being used by the Particular (Calvinistic) Baptists. The Assembly resolved to send William Strange, John Bishell and John Roberts, a Lincoln Baptist, to investigate the situation and report back to the next Assembly. These three men came up with what they considered to be an ingenious idea. They persuaded a friend, William Richards of King's Lynn, to visit Lincoln and make the necessary enquiries. Although William Richards had contact with the General Assembly, he was a hyper-Calvinist, and evidently his friends thought it a good idea to send a Calvinistic Baptist to speak to Calvinistic Baptists meeting in a leased (Old) General Baptist building. However, the idea turned out to be unsuccessful as William Richards was poorly received at Lincoln. The next Assembly recorded its thanks to him for his services, but added that they were sorry his efforts had been unsuccessful, and that they most sincerely regretted his treatment at Lincoln which, with some honourable exceptions, had been extremely illiberal, and utterly irreconcilable with the Spirit of Christianity.

---

2   General Baptists, not part of the New Connexion of General Baptists.

As far as the Assembly was concerned, the matter was closed, but not for the New Connexion of General Baptists. In 1819 they acquired the property of the Old General Baptists and the remainder of the agreement with the Particular Baptists. When the agreement expired in 1821 the buildings were let to the Congregationalists for a few months. In 1822 a new church was formed, becoming one of the New Connexion of General Baptists, and services resumed in the old buildings.

In 1824, a new Trust Deed was executed, but the church was very weak and struggling. In 1828 there were only twelve members, when Mr E. Kingsford, who had ministered to the church for the previous three years, was invited to become Pastor. Three deacons were appointed at the same time, and it is interesting to note that there must have been a meeting place 'up-hill', as the appointments were made by the church in Newport and St Benedict's Square.

Moving on to 1829, Mr S. Wright became Pastor, and it was reported that the congregations were moderately good, with a membership of thirty-four and a flourishing Sunday School. Services were also being held in Washingborough. In 1832, membership had fallen slightly to twenty-nine, but in 1836 the cause was reported to be improving. Mr Wright was ordained in 1838, and in the following year the church reported that membership had increased to forty-nine and there was 'unanimity and peace'.

Unfortunately, the 'peace' did not last. A dispute arose between Mr Wright and the Trustees concerning an old tenement, causing a division in the membership. Some took Mr Wright's side, others that of the Trustees, and the matter was referred to the Lincolnshire Association. Although there are no records of any decision, it is probable that the Association decided that the Trustees were correct, as in 1844 the church at Boston refused to transfer a member to Lincoln because of Mr Wright's action. At this point, the Lincoln church reported that 'our state is by no means prosperous'; there were forty-seven members, forty scholars in the Sunday School with six teachers. However, following this incident Mr Wright remained as Pastor for a further eight years, completing twenty-three years of ministry before resigning in 1852 due to ill health.

In the same year, Rev. John Crapps became Pastor and served until 1854. During this period the congregation had increased considerably, and were encouraged by the North Lincolnshire Conference to attempt to obtain a new chapel. However, by the time Mr Crapps withdrew from the pastorate in 1854 nothing had been done in this respect, and services were conducted by the former pastor, Mr Wright, assisted by Mr Ward, one of the deacons.

For a time, services were still held every Sunday, but the decline which had set in was evidently too serious for the dwindling membership to cope with and very soon it was resolved to meet for worship once a month only, when the Lord's Supper would also be observed. Eventually the few remaining members were called together and decided that because of the present situation, the chapel should be closed altogether. It now appeared likely, that after two centuries of struggle, which had seen both days of prosperity and adversity, the General Baptist cause in Lincoln was about to come to an end. But this was not to be – God had other plans. There were still a few who believed that this was not the end, and whose hopes and prayers were yet to be realised as we shall see.

Chapter 4

Rebuilding the church

*The reconstituted and rebuilt General Baptist Church
in the parish of St Benedict (1860 – 1885)*

Among the small number of members of the church when
the decision was taken to close the building were two devout
women – Ann Ashton and Rebecca Dayles. The others, who
apparently believed the cause was dead, joined the Mint Street
Particular Baptist Church. God had convinced these two
women that the General Baptist cause in Lincoln had not
ended and given them the hope that something would be
done to revive the church. Ann Ashton and Rebecca Dayles
refused to relinquish their membership and join another
church. So, even though the chapel was closed, there was still
a General Baptist church in Lincoln, albeit with only two
members, through whom its continuity was maintained.

One of the most interesting entries which was found in an
old Church Minute Book is the following statement:

Memorandum
That Ann Ashton and Rebecca Dayles never united with
any other Church, in the full hope and expectation that
some effort would be made by the General Baptist
Denomination for the resuscitation of the cause, as declared

by them in the old General Baptist Vestry, on the 3rd day of April, 1860.

[Signed] *John Penny and William Mitton*

At the Association meetings in Derby the previous year, it had been reported by the late Pastor, Mr Wright, that the cause was extinct, and in view of this report a further declaration was made and signed in the Church Minute Book as follows:

Memorandum

The account sent by the Rev. S. Wright to the Association Meeting in Derby and published in the Minutes of 1859 was not correct. The Church was not extinct as we, the undersigned, can testify.

[Signed] *William Mitton, Hannah Mitton, Ann Ashton [X her mark], Rebecca Dayles [X her mark]*

Witnessed by:

[Signed] *John Penny and William Bauser*

From these interesting statements it can be seen that the General Baptist church was never quite extinct. The hopes and prayers of Ann Ashton and Rebecca Dayles began to be realised as others joined them. Among those were John Penny, Ann Penny, James Penny, George Faulkner Muse and Amy Muse. These friends consulted together and in conjunction with the Rev. T. W. Matthews of Boston and the Rev. J. H. Wood of Sutterton, resolved to reconstitute the church. Accordingly, a meeting for this purpose was

Plaque commemorating Ann Ashton and Rebecca Dayles on the rear wall of TCM church held in the vestry of the old chapel on 3 April 1860. Rev. Matthews took the chair and Rev. Wood was also present. After much discussion the following statement was drawn up and signed:

> The General Baptist Church meeting in the parish of St Benedict, Lincoln, having become reduced to two members, namely: Ann Ashton and Rebecca Dayles, we the undersigned baptised believers, do agree to unite with them in Church Fellowship, and with the approbation of the Trustees of the said Chapel, and also of T. W. Matthews, pastor of the General Baptist Church at Boston, and J. H. Wood, pastor of the General Baptist Church at Sutterton, do hereby constitute ourselves a Church of the Lord Jesus Christ, for maintaining fellowship with each other, observing the ordinances of the Lord's appointment, extending by all the suitable efforts the Kingdom or our Lord and Saviour, and exercising such discipline as is enjoined in the Holy Scriptures for the purity of the Church of Christ.
>
> [Signed] *Ann Penny, John Penny, James Penny, William Mitton, William Rowlatt, George Faulkner Muse, Amy Muse, Hannah Pfiel, Ann Revill*

George Muse was appointed to act as secretary, and William Mitton as treasurer. Following these procedures all the members partook of the Lord's Supper.

For a time, the reconstituted church worshipped in the house of George Faulkner Muse, as the chapel building was in a very dilapidated condition, although it was then being used as a Ragged school.[1] As numbers began to grow it

---

1 Ragged schools were charitable organisations dedicated to the free education of destitute children in nineteenth-century Britain. The schools were developed in working-class districts of the rapidly expanding industrial towns.

became impractical to continue meeting in a private house, and so services were held in the Corn Exchange (now a retail shopping centre in the Cornhill area of Lincoln).

In May 1860, the church was received back into the General Baptist Association, and only two months after reforming, a special Church Meeting was held to consider the advisability of approaching the Trustees of the property with a proposal to rebuild the chapel. Although permission was granted, services were never again held in the old chapel, and for the time being the church continued to meet for worship in the Corn Exchange.

In August 1860, three Deacons were appointed: William Bauser, George Faulkner Muse and John Penny. The year 1860 was therefore a very important year in the history of the church, prompting John Penny to write in the Church Minute Book on 31 December, 1860, 'Surely goodness and mercy hath followed us.'

A Sunday School was opened on 3 March 1861 and scholars enrolled, one of whom was George Hood. George Hood was a young man destined to hold every office in the church, except that of pastor, and lived long enough to celebrate fifty years of church membership.[2] The 31 March 1861, was a day of great blessing for the church. At the morning service the Rev. J. Greenwood of Nottingham baptised George Hood and five others. In the afternoon, the Rev. T. W. Matthews of Boston baptised four others, and at the evening Communion service all those who had been baptised were welcomed into membership.

In July 1861, a building committee was formed to consider plans for the new chapel, and in October of that year the church agreed that it was right to hold 'Open Communion',

2   (see p. 80).

for all believers to commemorate the Lord's death, whether baptised or not. The design for the new chapel was adopted in the following year, 1862, which, considering their small number, was a great step of faith. An earlier entry in the Church Minute Book, however, gives us an insight into the spirit in which the members undertook this commitment. It states:

February 12th 1861
In relation to the new Chapel it was resolved:
1. That all members should give something.
2. That all give as God hath enabled them.
3. That all give willingly.
4. That we attempt great things for God and expect great things from Him.

In May 1863, the church invited the Rev. John Cookson of Boston, USA, to become Pastor with the modest stipend of £70 a year. Mr Cookson accepted the invitation and ministered to the church for ten years before the Lord called him home.

The church prospered. Prayer meetings and week night services were held in the vestry of the old chapel before it was finally pulled down. The foundation stones for the new chapel were laid on 18 August 1863, and the original Baptist Chapel with its cottages in the front disappeared for ever. There is no known record in picture form of the old home of the Lincoln General Baptists, but Mr George Hood described it at the time as follows:

St Benedict Lane, as its name was in 1860, would not be recognised with the square of today. Memory sees the old Church, with its graveyard surrounded by an old, high wall, half hiding the then disused building. A narrow lane on either

side, so narrow that only one vehicle could go down at once.
A row of low, whitewashed thatched cottages on the north
side and three small tenements at the west end facing up the
lane, two of which hid the original Chapel. The Chapel itself
was reached by a wooden door giving entrance to a narrow
passage leading to the open yard behind the two tenements,
which formed part of the Chapel property. The Chapel itself
was a plain brick building, facing east to west, with a door at
each end and a single aisle the whole length of the Chapel
with pews at each side, the pulpit being at the west end and
close to the door. Behind this was a small graveyard,
occasionally occupied by a few sheep grazing, and used as
a drying ground on wash days.

When completed, the new sanctuary was a somewhat larger
building facing St Benedict's Square, and for the first time could
be seen from the High Street. A vestry with a schoolroom
above was built at the rear, but most of the graveyard was still

Plaque in memory to Rev. John Cookson
on the rear wall of TCM church

left as an open space. These
buildings continued to serve
the church until 1885, when
they also were taken down to
make way for a beautiful
building which would be
known later as the Thomas
Cooper Memorial Church –
but we must not jump ahead.

During a Church Meeting
held on the 19 April 1871 the
news was brought that John
Penny had passed away. The
minutes of the meeting recorded that the announcement
'brought a solemn impression on all present'. His death

was a great loss to the church. He had been a Deacon since the formation of the church in 1860 and, together with his wife (better known as Mrs Mears), had been chiefly instrumental in directing the little church in the steps they took. But for their constant cheerfulness and guidance the progress made would have been impossible. Prior to his death, John Penny had been suffering from a painful illness for about six years and confined to his room for much of this time.

The following year, 1872, John Penny's widow presented the church with a beautiful Communion Set. Another member, Mr Height, presented a Communion Table. A large chair was presented by Mr J. Lambert and two smaller matching chairs were presented by Mrs Height and Mrs Hawson. (At the time of writing, all of these items of furniture are stored in our present building.)

Under the care and ministry of the Pastor, Rev. John Cookson, the church grew numerically and spiritually. Following his death in the spring of 1873, Rev. E. Compton became Pastor in the autumn of the same year, and served the church for nine years. During his ministry Mr George Hood became a Deacon in 1876, and in the same year, Thomas Cooper (see Appendix 1) became a member of the church by transfer from Commercial Road, London. He had been baptised by the Rev. J. F. Winks, in Friar Lane Baptist Church, Leicester, on Whit Sunday, 1859.

In 1881, Mr George Hood became Church Secretary, and during the same year Thomas Cooper frequently preached in the chapel to crowded congregations. The following year, 1882, Rev. Compton resigned the pastorate and at a farewell meeting was presented with a gift of £20 from the church. Addresses were given by the Rev. J. Williamson of Newland Congregational Church and the Rev. G. P. Mackay of Mint

The reconstituted and rebuilt General Baptist Church
in the parish of St Benedict

Street Baptist Church, both being well known ministers in their respective denominations.

A student from Nottingham College, whose name is not recorded, became Pastor from June 1882 until July 1885. About this time the church began to feel the necessity to either alter the premises to meet its growing requirements or to erect a new building – the latter course was decided upon. At the Annual General Church Meeting held on 1 January, 1884, Mr G. F. Muse proposed that when erected the new building should be called the Thomas Cooper Memorial Church. This was unanimously agreed to, and Thomas Cooper gave his consent. At this time the fund for this purpose amounted to £55.

Chapter 5

Thomas Cooper Memorial Church (Part 1)

St Benedict's Square

Having decided upon the new building, the members put a great deal of effort into implementing their decision and raising the necessary funds. A bazaar, that probably today we would have called a car boot sale, was held in the Corn Exchange bringing in £210, which together with subscriptions and monies raised by other means, increased the new building fund to £640.

The last services were held in the old chapel on 22 March 1885, and in the same week plans were adopted and contracts signed for the erection of a building costing £3,000. The plans were drawn up by Mr J. Wallis Chapman, an architect and a Deacon at Dr John Clifford's[1] church in Westbourne Park, London, and included taking down the old chapel and rebuilding it behind the new one for use as a Sunday School. Doing so meant the old building overlooked the Brayford Pool and served as a monument to the members of the little church of 1860, who built it and freed it from debt.

The new church, meeting hall and classrooms, covered the

---

1 John Clifford was a prominent leader of the Baptist Church in England, becoming, in turn, the President of the London Baptist Union (1879), the National Baptist Union (1888) and the Baptist World Alliance.

whole of the original site and included an additional portion of land purchased and given by Mrs Mears, the widow of John Penny. She also purchased a third cottage and handed it and the portion of land that went with it over to the Trustees. A further portion of land, on the south side, was purchased by the Trustees themselves.

The foundation stones were laid on Easter Monday, 6 April, 1885, one by Dr Clifford, one by Mr G. F. Muse representing the Sunday School and the church of 1860, one by Mr G. Hood on behalf of the church, and others by such leading citizens as Mr Henry Newsum JP, Alderman J. Maltby JP and Mr John Richardson JP (see Appendix 4). A memorial stone to the late Mr John Penny was placed in the centre by Mrs Mears.

The new church was opened on the 2 May, 1886. Thomas Cooper preached the opening sermons on that day and contributed £50 out of his literary earnings to the collection. It is also interesting to note that contributions to the building fund had been received from friends of Thomas Cooper, such as the Rt Hon. A. J. Mundella MP, Mr Joseph Cowen MP, Mr W. S. Caine MP and Mr G. J. Holyoake.[2] By the time the church was opened, some £2,000 had been raised towards the cost, regarded as something of a miracle.

The first minister of the church in its new home was the Rev. John Ebenezer Bennett who began his ministry in December 1886. At that time there were 109 members of the church, facing an outstanding sum of £1,100 for the cost of the building. Mr George Hood wrote about Rev. Bennett's ministry as follows:

---

2 George Jacob Holyoake was a British secularist and an old colleague of Thomas Cooper. He persuaded the Gladstone Cabinet to grant Thomas Cooper a pension of £300 (given in three annual instalments to prevent him giving too much of it away!). In 1887, George Holyoake was President of the Co-operative Congress.

Mr Bennett's ministry continued for seven and a half years, and was a record of untiring and devoted service in the City generally and to the Church. Mr Bennett was a faithful minister of Jesus Christ, in season and out of season, a real expositor of the revealed Will of God, taking his hearers through consecutive books of the Old and New Testaments. During his ministry the Church reached the highest point of prosperity yet attained, and the Sunday School had the largest number of teachers and scholars ever recorded in its books. The debt on the Church buildings . . . was reduced to £350, and an organ was added in 1889 at the cost of £200, making a total liability of £550. This has since been reduced by £200, Mrs Mears presenting the Church with a cheque for that amount shortly before her death in 1910.

Our contributions to foreign missions reached a high-water mark, being no less than £29 3s 3d for that year. Mr Bennett's ministry awakened a new enthusiasm in our Church life: he discovered amongst its younger members many whom he trained in Church work, encouraging them to take service in different departments and assume the responsibility of office. Two of these are now in the Baptist ministry, namely: Rev. Robert Martin (with his devoted wife, also one of our former Sunday School scholars, and daughter of the late G. F. Muse), and the Rev. Edgar Jackson. Others served the Church faithfully and with zeal, such as Mr John Hayes, Mr F. Bryant and Mr H. Willerton.[3]

During the Rev. Bennett's ministry, Thomas Cooper was called home on 15 July 1892 at the age of 87. He was buried

---

3 A few minor changes have been made to the original text to improve readability.

in the Canwick Road Cemetery, Lincoln, in the same grave as his wife Susanna, who was called home on 1 February 1880.

In May, 1894, Rev. Bennett ended his ministry in Lincoln to take up the pastorate of Mare Street Baptist Church, Hackney, London. Unfortunately, his health soon began to deteriorate and he died at Clacton-on-Sea three years later. After his death, many of his stories were published in a book, *Lights on Life, or, Short Stories of Christian Conduct* (with an introduction by Dr John Clifford). It includes a biographical sketch by Edward Hall Jackson, a former Baptist minister in Louth, and an old friend of Rev. Bennett and the church. Rev. Bennett's memoirs were also written by E. H. Jackson.

The Rev. Bennett was succeeded by the Rev. Frederick Arthur Jackson in January 1895, who ministered to the church until December 1901. He was a pastor of remarkable ability, and his sermons were masterpieces, the outcome of quiet thought and meditation. His ministry also demonstrated that he possessed a rare poetic gift, which later resulted in a volume of songs being published under the title *Just Beyond and Other Poems*. He also published a volume of his addresses entitled *Noiseless Buildings*. Because of his personality, Rev. Jackson made many friends and when he left Lincoln he was held in high regard by the church and many in the city.

The following year, in June 1902, the Rev. Frank E. Miller, one of Dr Clifford's students, accepted the vacant pastorate. He served the Lord faithfully in the church for six years before resigning in 1908. Rev. Miller was a very optimistic man and demonstrated great enthusiasm in his ministry. His preaching was of a very high standard, the result of careful study and the ability of a thoroughly trained mind.[4]

---

4 Rev. Miller's letter of resignation, the church's response and tributes to his ministry are recorded in the Minutes of Church Meetings for 16 March, 1908, and 7 September 1908.

Thomas Cooper Memorial Church (TCM), St Benedict's Square

Thomas Cooper Memorial Church (TCM); rear view from Brayford showing rebuilt old church
(Photograph courtesy of Lincolnshire Archives)

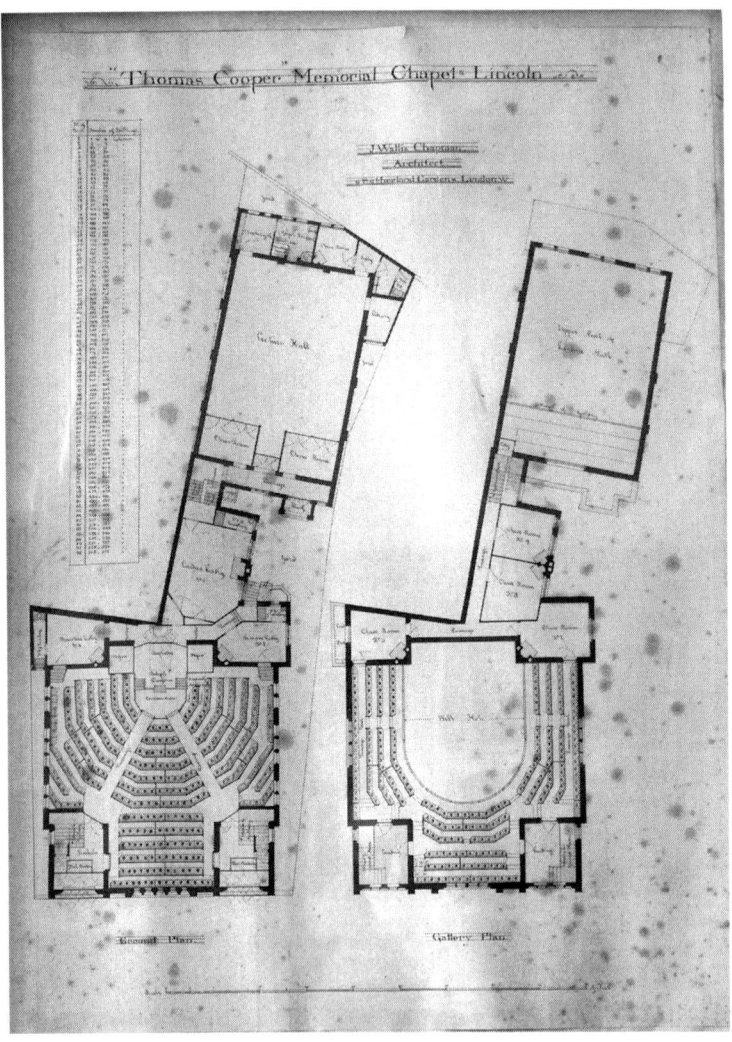

Plans for Thomas Cooper Memorial Church, St Benedict's Square
prepared by architect J. Wallis Chapman

Inside views of Thomas Cooper Memorial Church,
St Benedict's Square

It seems that the church was then without a pastor for two years, until the Rev. R. T. Anderson was appointed and began his ministry on Sunday, 6 March 1910. The Minutes of Church Meetings for the intervening period record that members of the Diaconate presided at Church Meetings and were responsible for arrangements to fill the pulpit for the Sunday services. In particular, Mr Willerton, the Sunday School Superintendent, Mr John Hayes and Mr W. S. Linton had important roles during this period.

Early in 1911 the church celebrated George Hood's 'Jubilee of Church Membership'. The Minutes of the Church Meeting for 20 February, 1911, record the contents of a letter to George Hood expressing the church's appreciation of his fifty years membership and faithful service to the church. The occasion was marked by a celebration on Tuesday, 18 April, when Dr John Clifford was the preacher. A large number of people were present, including representatives from the majority of Lincoln churches and public figures. Newspaper reports of the event appeared in *The Lincolnshire Echo* and *The Lincoln Leader*.[5]

Later in the year, the health of Rev. Anderson gave cause for concern, and the church agreed to grant him a three-month holiday in which to recover, and continued to pay his salary during this time. At a Special Church Meeting in February, 1912, the Church Secretary read a letter received from Rev. Anderson, stating that he intended to relinquish the pastorate in March as he had accepted an invitation to another church in Leighton Buzzard. His resignation was accepted with regret, and Rev. Anderson finished his ministry on Sunday, 31 March, 1912.

---

5 The Minutes of Church Meetings for April, 1911, contain an article from *The Lincoln Leader*, published on 22 April, 1911 and include a photograph of the event, which, despite the poor quality, is reproduced in Appendix 4, together with the article from *The Lincolnshire Echo*.

An offer from the Rev. Sidney Bowser, Principal of the Nottingham College, for Mr Claud M. Coltman to become the student pastor for a six-month term was accepted in September, 1912. Although Mr Coltman was invited to continue the arrangement at the end of the term, the college Principal reduced Mr Coltman's involvement to once a month as he had an important examination to prepare for in June.

After several attempts to fill the pastorate on a permanent basis, the Rev. Charles H. Homer of Beeston, Nottinghamshire, accepted an invitation, and began his ministry on Sunday, 6 September, 1914.

During the war years great difficulties were encountered in maintaining church services and other activities. The School Room was used by the military authorities to billet soldiers, dark nights and lighting restrictions resulted in attendance at services being uncertain, food restrictions prevented any of the usual functions being held, there was a great deal of sickness, and young people were leaving the church. Church members were encouraged by the pastor to pray earnestly about the situation and attend weekly nights of prayer.

Difficulties continued after the war and the membership continued to decline. There were also financial problems resulting from essential repair bills, and the general condition of the church building was poor.

In passing, it's interesting to note that at a Church Meeting held on 27 February, 1919, it was decided to elect two lady deacons at the next Church Meeting 'with the hope of widening the interests and increasing the usefulness of members', and two ladies were duly appointed on 27 March, 1919. However, the minutes of the Annual Meeting of Members held on 14 January, 1920, record that 'one refused the office and the other did not like to come without the other'.

After six years of ministry, Rev. Homer announced his decision in February, 1920, not to continue for a further period and to finish his ministry in August of that year.

During the remaining months of his ministry, Rev. Homer presided over a number of Church Meetings regarding the future of the church. The issue was first raised at a Special Church Meeting held on 20 May, 1920, when the following notice was read to the church members:

> Notice is hereby given that a Meeting of the Trustees and Members of the Congregation and all other persons interested or claiming to be interested in the Thomas Cooper Memorial Chapel situate at St Benedict's Square, Lincoln, will be held on Thursday the 20th day of May 1920 at 7 o'clock precisely for the purpose of considering an application proposed to be made to the Board of Charity Commissioners for England and Wales for authority to sell the property in St Benedict's Square and authorise the proceeds of the sale to be laid out in the purchase of a suitable site and the erection of a new chapel in a desirable part of Lincoln.
> (Church Minutes, 20 May, 1920)

When Rev. Homer finished his ministry on 29 August, 1920, this matter was still ongoing. However, by the time the Church Meeting held on 12 January, 1921, took place three new Trustees had been appointed, and the Trustees had applied for powers to dispose of the church property when thought fit to do so by the members.

Without a pastor, the future of the church became increasingly uncertain and the number of members decreased. The decision was taken to hold only one service on a Sunday evening and to let part of the premises during the week in order to provide some much needed income. Meetings were held with the officers of Mint Street and Monks Road Baptist churches and the Lincoln Free Church Council to discuss the future of Baptists in Lincoln, and help with the pulpit supply was sought from the members of the Mint Street Church.

The minutes of a Church Meeting held on 18 April, 1921, record that the Trustees had acquired the necessary authority to sell the property, subject to the approval of the membership, and the Trust Deeds had been amended accordingly. Approval from the membership to empower the Trustees to sell the church premises at the most favourable opportunity was given at a Church Meeting held on 25 April 1921.

On a positive note, despite the declining membership and the problems facing the church, an active Sunday School had been maintained due to the faithful and energetic efforts of Mr H. Willerton and Mr A. Wilson. Although the church premises had not been sold, by October 1922 a mere handful of members remained, and it seemed that the light which had burned in Lincoln for three hundred years was about to be extinguished. Dark days had once again fallen on the church whose witness had been maintained through three centuries, and it seemed now was the time for the final curtain to be rung down. But, yet again, there were one or two dauntless souls who believed that the end was not yet, and clung on to their belief that God still had a work to do through the Thomas Cooper Memorial Church, as we shall now go on to see.

Chapter 6

Thomas Cooper Memorial Church (Part 2)

The Thomas Cooper Memorial Mission

In October 1922, all past and present members of Thomas Cooper Memorial Church were invited to attend a Church Meeting at which a final decision was to be made regarding the future of the church. One of those present was a former member and Deacon, Mr W. H. Radford, who was well received and lovingly welcomed. Largely because of his suggestions, it was decided to attempt to establish the work once again, but on a completely new basis which would start with a Campaign. Another former member, his son, Mr Cecil H. Radford, accepted an invitation to become the Campaign Secretary, an undertaking for which he was well qualified.

As a result of this decision, the Church Secretary, Mr A. Tuck, sent a letter to the Rev. T. Nightingale, the Secretary of the Free Church Council in London, enquiring if he knew of a man who would come to Lincoln to hold a month's Campaign. The letter to Mr Nightingale arrived at the same time as a letter from Rev. R. S. Bradbrook, a Baptist Evangelist, who had just returned from America and who was open to accept engagements. The power of God was at work!

Rev. Bradbrook was interviewed and informed about the church's situation. He felt that coming to lead the Campaign was a true call from God. It presented a challenge, which he accepted, and together with Mr Cecil H. Radford planned what was to become the start of an outstanding and fruitful ministry.

At this point, the church premises were in a very poor state and there were no funds. There was no adequate heating, no electric lighting in the balcony, the organ was practically unplayable, and the only piano on the premises had been borrowed and was not available for the new venture. To make matters even worse, very few of the chairs and other seats in the schoolrooms and vestries were serviceable.

Undaunted, and believing in the God of the impossible, the Campaign Secretary, Mr Radford, began work in November, 1922, arranging everything to enable the Mission (as it became known) to begin in February the following year. Gas radiators were fitted, the organ was temporarily repaired, electric lighting was installed, new hymnbooks were purchased, and a piano was hired.

On Sunday, 11 February, 1923, the evening service was led by a local Methodist preacher, Mr J. T. Waite, who faithfully continued to provide help and support during the early days of the Mission. This was followed by a week of prayer prior to the opening of the Mission on Sunday, 18 February, when Rev. Bradbrook began his ministry. By all accounts, these were wonderful meetings – the Thomas Cooper Memorial Mission was founded on prayer.

On the day of the opening there was a foot of snow on the ground but, despite the weather, at 5.30 pm a faithful group held an open-air meeting at the corner of St Benedict's Square before the 6.00 pm service. Following the service at 8.00 pm, a 'Song Service' was held and crowds came to see what it would be like.

In those days, as there were no other attractions on Sundays, and no other churches in Lincoln holding late evening meetings, these Song Services continued Sunday by Sunday, until April, 1937 (when they continued in the open air), and were the beginning of a great ministry through song. The singing was accompanied by a small orchestra formed by Mr C. Chapell, who sadly was called home in 1930. He was an expert trombone player, who attended practically every meeting, and it is recorded that,

> [he] joyfully helped the praise of the singers. It was an inspiration to behold his beaming face. His heart and soul were in his playing, and if ever a man 'made a joyful noise unto the Lord' it was our dear brother . . .
> (*These Five and Twenty Years*, p. 8)

Many others contributed to the work and success of the Mission in those early days. The services of a few were particularly outstanding and deserve a mention. Mr H. Green, the editor of the weekly paper the *Lincoln Leader*, was a staunch supporter, his encouragement providing a great stimulus. He gave of his time and made space in the paper for 'write-ups' which were of untold help. Miss Gladys Green ably and efficiently coped with huge amount of administrative work involved. Mr Fred Martin was a talented pianist, whose brilliant playing took the singing to a new level.

In 1923, young people in the Mission were participating in the Young Life Campaign (YLC), a youth evangelism movement started in 1911 by Arthur and Frederick Wood. In 1924 a YLC meeting was held at the Lincoln Drill Hall, where new songs were learnt from the *Young Life Campaign Hymn Book*, under the direction of Mr Fred Martin. These proved to be a great attraction to the crowds of young people who became associated with this work, and the church was very much encouraged by the presence of a party of Campaigners who came over from Nottingham.

During the first two months of the Mission, meetings were held each night, and there were many converts. God was moving! These were great days of campaigning.

Another innovation was the Saturday evening 'Happy Hour', a meeting that continued for many years.

Owing to sickness, Rev. Bradbrook was unable to preach at several meetings during one week, and his place was taken by the organising secretary, Mr C. H. Radford. God graciously honoured his ministry with a number of conversions.

On 19 April, 1923, Mr C. H. Radford was appointed Honorary Pastor to assist Rev. Bradbrook, who had agreed to remain until the end of April. Following the departure of Rev. Bradbrook, Mr Radford continued to act in this capacity.

Significant numbers of people were now being added to the Mission each week, many of whom were baptised. However, there were also numerous critics, and opposition appeared from the most unexpected quarters. The Mission's stand for the fundamental truths of the gospel attracted many scornful comments, and it was publicly said that the revival was only 'a flash in the pan'. Courage was drawn from the words of Gamaliel in Acts chapter 5, regarding the work of the apostles:

'. . . leave these men alone! Let them go! For if their purpose
or activity is of human origin, it will fail. But if it is from God,
you will not be able to stop these men; you will only find
yourselves fighting against God.'
(Acts 5:38–39, NIV)

At this time the Mission was a separate body holding its meetings in the Thomas Cooper Memorial Church (TCM) with the permission of the Trustees. Discussions were held between the Deacons and Trustees of TCM, and Mr C. H. Radford regarding the future of TCM and the Mission. At a Special Church Meeting on 20 November, 1924, it was resolved:

> That we, the members of the TCM Church, heartily approve the great work of the Mission, and agree that it should continue, subject to a satisfactory arrangement re the TCM membership being arrived at.

The suggested arrangement was:

> that a sufficient number of baptised believers be added to the Church Roll from time to time to maintain a Baptist Church in order to satisfy the requirements of the Trust Deed, and that the present Mission be carried on nominally by the Church, without necessarily effecting any change in the work.

The minutes of a subsequent meeting on 28 November, 1924, record that a provisional agreement had been reached, subject to the approval of the TCM members and baptised Mission members:

> that while no pressure should be put upon any member of the Mission to be baptised, or upon baptised members of the Mission to the join the TCM Church Roll, a cordial invitation be given through Mr Radford to baptised members of the Mission to join the Church Roll for the purpose of perpetuating a membership which alone could secure the continuance of the Mission in the TCM Church premises . . . The baptised

members, being the Church, with the cooperation of all active members of the Mission, would take over full financial responsibility for the buildings.

After a brief discussion, the following resolution was passed:

That this meeting of the TCM Church approve the report of the Joint Committee, and notes with satisfaction that many members will be added to the list of baptised believers, and welcomes into fellowship all active members of the Mission.

According to a report given by Mr Radford to a Meeting of Members of Thomas Cooper Memorial Mission held on 4 December, 1924, an Active Members' Covenant drawn up by the Mission had been signed by 176 members, 30 of whom had been baptised. Mr Radford then outlined the provisional agreement which had been reached and submitted the above resolution to the members for their consideration. After a short discussion the following resolution was passed:

That this meeting wishes to place on record its great appreciation of the work of Mr C. H. Radford in negotiating the above matter and fully approves of the steps which he has taken to bring it to a satisfactory settlement.

The fusion between TCM Baptist Church and the Mission was complete, and at the same meeting the appointment of Mr Cecil H. Radford as the Honorary Pastor was unanimously approved. It was a memorable meeting.

By this time the work of Mission had grown considerably from almost nothing, and included the following weekly meetings:

Sunday	9.45 am	Sunday School
	10.30 am	Morning service
	2.00 pm	Sunday School
	3.00 pm	Bible class
	6.00 pm	Evening service
	8.00 pm	Song service
Tuesday	6.15 pm	Children's meeting
	7.15 pm	Prayer meeting
Wednesday	3.00 pm	Women's meeting
	7.15 pm	Young people's rally
Thursday	7.15 pm	Choir practice
Saturday	7.15 pm	Happy Hour

Several organisations had also been started: a Scout Troop and Cub Pack for boys, a Guide Company for girls, and a Women's Auxilary which arranged teas and visited 400 homes each month delivering tracts. During the winter months a training class for young people was held.

A Canteen was open every Saturday evening, which before World War II was a very popular venue, selling chocolates, sweets and cakes of all descriptions. Lean times during in the war and while there was rationing in the following years, meant that the Canteen was only able to provide a cup of tea or coffee and a very plain cake. However, it was always a meeting place on a Saturday night for those attending the Happy Hour and a place where many friendships were made, including the beginning of some 'happy matches'.

The combined work and witness of the TCM Church and the Mission that was established under Mr Cecil H. Radford in 1924 continued to flourish throughout his thirty-five years of ministry, and has remained the basis of TCM's Christian witness in Lincoln, the surrounding area, and other parts of the world ever since. We will now go on to highlight some of the significant work and witness of TCM, and changes and events that have taken place over the years since then.

Thomas Cooper Memorial Church, St Benedict's Square
(view from the Garden of Rest, photo courtesy of *Lincolnshire Echo*)

Chapter 7

Thomas Cooper Memorial Church (Part 3)

Significant work, witness, changes and events since 1924

It is not the purpose of this book to give a detailed account of all the work and witness of TCM or the changes and events that have taken place since 1924. Specific details can be found in the minutes of Church Meetings, newspaper articles and other documents if required. However, there are some significant aspects that are now covered in this chapter.

An unchanging witness

TCM's witness – to the eternal existence and uniqueness of the triune God as Father, Son and Holy Spirit; to Jesus Christ as fully God and fully man, and in whom alone forgiveness of sin, salvation and eternal life are available; to the Holy Spirit, who convicts sinners, indwells believers imparting spiritual life, understanding of the Scriptures and empowerment for service; and to the inerrancy of the Bible as the inspired Word of God through which He is revealed – has remained unchanged over the years.[1] Faithful preaching from the Word of God, without compromise, and the Lordship of Jesus

---

1   See the TCM Constitution for a full doctrinal statement of belief.

Christ have always been hallmarks of TCM's witness and ministry.

TCM Pastors and Assistants since 1924

Pastors

After thirty-five years of ministry at TCM, Pastor Cecil H. Radford finally retired on 31 March,1958. Some biographical details and a tribute written by a church member at the time, are given in Appendix 2.

In 1959, the Rev. Harry Whyte, who had been the Pastor at Stockton Baptist Tabernacle for a number of years, was called to the pastorate, and occupied the newly-acquired manse.[2] His induction service took place on Saturday, 13 June, and he faithfully preached the gospel until April, 1963, before he moved to Bristol to become the Pastor of City Road, Baptist Church.

For a short time TCM was without a pastor once again. During this period visiting preachers and very capable men in the church conducted Sunday services. Assistance was also sought from Harold Watson, who was well known and much loved by TCM members. After prayerful consideration, he agreed to come and help for a period of time. Harold Watson spent much time studying the Word of God and was a passionate preacher, using many anecdotes and stories in his sermons. His pastoral ministry was second to none, and as he did not drive he walked many miles around Lincoln visiting people. Towards the end of 1965 he completed his period of assistance at TCM, but prior to leaving he recommended Rev. J. T. Orrell as a possible future pastor.

---

2   The first manse was at 192 West Parade and sold shortly after Rev. Orrell left TCM. The current manse at 19 West Drive, Sudbrooke, was purchased in 1995 and first occupied by Rev. Roy Bedford.

Rev. J. T. Orrell was a Lancashire man, born in Hindley Green on 29 June, 1930. He was converted in his early teens while attending Central Hall Mission Church, Westhoughton, Bolton, and led many gospel outreach missions. Having been called to the ministry, he trained in Surrey and became an acredited minister with the Federation of Independent Evangelical Churches (FIEC). He had served in a pastorate in Liverpool, but in 1965 Rev. Orrell was settled and happy in his ministry as the Pastor of Pennygate Evangelical Church in Spalding. However, as a result of the recommendation from Harold Watson, Rev. Orrell was invited to come and preach at TCM, and subsequently accepted a call to the pastorate. His induction service was held on Saturday, 30 April, 1966 and he remained as Pastor until September,1984. In November, he moved to Canada, where he had relatives, to take up further ministry. He departed to Christ's presence on 10 January, 2013, in King City, Ontario, and a memorial service was held on 16 January. During his pastorate TCM moved from St Benedict's Square to the High Street (see p. 107), and he established an eldership as part of the church leadership (see p. 100).

In 1987, Rev. James K. McClatchey was called of God to the pastorate of TCM and his induction service was held on Saturday, 2 January, 1988. Rev. McClatchey was born in Northern Ireland and was employed by Rolls Royce in Belfast as an aero engineer, before leaving in 1970 to train at the Irish Baptist College. He began his ministry in Killicomaine Evangelical Church, Portadown, Northern Ireland, then moved to Bethany Evangelical Church, Leigh, in Lancashire. In December, 1982, he moved to Hope Hall Evangelical Church in Paisley, Scotland, and in 1985 he was President of the FIEC. He remained Pastor of TCM until 1994.

In 1995, Rev. Roy Bedford became Pastor and remained until 1999. Roy came to know the Lord Jesus Christ as his personal

Saviour in November 1969 at a Campaign in Cape Town, South Africa. Between 1974 and 1980 he did financial and administrative studies and worked in financial banking and as company secretary for Barlow Rand Gold Mining Group. In 1981, Roy sensed God's call on his life into full-time ministry, and after confirmation by godly men, he underwent training at the Baptist Theological College of Southern Africa, where he graduated with Licentiate in Theology (with honours), after four years' full-time study. Confirmation of his call has subsequently come through seeing God at work in people's lives in the pastorates in which he has served. Prior to coming to TCM, Roy pastored three Baptist Union churches in South Africa: Pietermaritzburg Central Baptist Church (1985–1989), Grahamstown Baptist Church (1989–1993) and Beacon Bay Baptist Church, East London (1993–1995). Highlights during his pastorate at TCM included the week-long Luis Palau campaign in 1998 during which many lives were changed and a closer working together of the churches brought about, growth and development in all aspects of church life, the conversion and baptism of many young people, introduction of the current TCM logo/branding, giving the church a fresh identity, and mission trips to Romania (see p. 122). After leaving TCM, Roy has pastored at Peacehaven Evangelical Free Church, UK (2000–2005), Kloof Baptist Church, South Africa (2005–2008), and since 2009 has been the Pastor of Warminster Baptist Church in Wiltshire. In 2012, Roy graduated with a Masters degree in Ministry and has a desire to help train pastors in Africa where they have not had the opportunity of seminary training.

Rev. Hugh Hill became Pastor of TCM in 2000; his induction service was held on 23 September. Hugh was born and brought up in Glasgow in a traditional liberal Church of Scotland family. In 1955, Hugh went forward in response to Billy Graham's invitation at Ibrox Park. However, although the

Pastor Cecil H. Radford

Rev. Harry Whyte

Rev. J. T. (Tom) Orrell

Rev. James K. McClatchey

Rev. Roy Bedford

Rev. Hugh Hill

Rev. Mike Smailes

Richard Wardman – *Assistant Pastor*   Andrew Miller – *Pastoral Assistant*

experience was genuine, he fell away and devoted himself to pursuing a sales career in print and packaging until a dramatic 'Damascus Road' experience in 1982 brought him back to the Lord. Recognising Jesus as 'Chairman' of his printing company brought about a number of miraculous events, which led to him joining CPO in Worthing and worshipping at Worthing Tabernacle. It was here that he received the 'call' to a full-time preaching ministry. Hugh attended London Theological Seminary for two years while pastoring Maybridge Christian Fellowship in Worthing. In 1992, he was called to the Slade Evangelical Church in Plumstead, South East London, and served there for eight years before finally moving to TCM. He retired in September 2007, and at present travels widely, helping churches concentrate on mission and growth. Currently, he has also written and published two books: *I Did It His Way*, and *A Journey through the Bible* (now published as *The Heart of the Bible* by Monarch Books).

In 2008, Rev. Mike Smailes became Pastor; his induction service was held on 26 January. From an early age Mike felt a strong sense of a call to serve the Lord in full-time ministry, and started his training by undertaking a correspondence course, while teaching chemistry and attending Kensington Baptist Church, Bristol, where he became a Pastoral Assistant. In 2001, he moved to Dunstable and served as Assistant Pastor at West Street Baptist Church. He continued his training by attending the Proclamation Trust Cornhill Training Course and Moore College. During Mike's pastorate, a fund was set up to assist in the training of those whose call into full-time ministry had been recognised by the church. To date, the fund has been used to support Richard Wardman and Andrew Miller (see below). After becoming Pastor of TCM, Mike served until 2013, when he resigned due to ill health.

Assistant Pastor – Richard Wardman

Richard came to Lincoln as a student in 1999 and was converted to Christ in his final year. He attended TCM while Hugh Hill was the Pastor, and after being lovingly nurtured and discipled as a new believer, Richard was baptised in 2003, welcomed into membership and married to Amy.

At that time, a few students were attending TCM, and Richard and Amy were asked to establish a student ministry. This grew quickly, and within a year some 25–30 students had made TCM their local church. As relatively new Christians, this presented a challenge, and they were asked by the elders to consider some Bible and ministry training, which, although they were unaware of it at the time, was the beginning of their training for full-time ministry. After attending FIEC's Prepared for Service course for two years, Richard was appointed as a full-time Pastoral Assistant at TCM, enabling him to gain valuable experience in preaching and leading under Hugh's mentorship.

Following Hugh's retirement in 2007, Mike Smailes continued to mentor Richard, furthering his development as a preacher and leader. In 2009, the church formally recognised his calling and appointed him as their first Assistant Pastor. Two years of formal theological training at Wales Evangelical School of Theology (WEST) followed, after which Richard continued to serve TCM until 2013, when he accepted a call to lead a church in Milton Keynes.

As well as the huge privilege of seeing many people saved and baptised over the years, a highlight of Richard's time at TCM was overseeing *Hope 2012*. This was a week-long mission, when TCM partnered with a church from Mississippi who sent a team of twelve people to assist in proclaiming the gospel at events in and around Lincoln.

Pastoral Assistant – Andrew Miller

Andrew came to faith in the Lord Jesus in childhood, and met his wife, Sarah, at a Christian youth camp. They were married in 2006 and set up home in Lincoln where Sarah was at university. Together, they attended TCM and served the Lord in various ministries. After working as a reporter on a local newspaper in Newark, Andrew became Pastoral Assistant at TCM, and was supported by the church while attending the Proclamation Trust Cornhill Training Course for two days a week in response to a call to full-time ministry. During the rest of the week, Andrew faithfully served TCM and developed his preaching gift under the mentoring of Mike Smailes and Hugh Hill. In 2010, Andrew began preaching at Newark Evangelical Church (NEC) as a visiting speaker. An on-going relationship with NEC developed, which in February, 2015, resulted in Andrew's ordination and induction as Assistant Pastor at NEC.

TCM leadership and affiliations

Church leadership at TCM comprised the Pastor, supported by Deacons, until Elders were appointed by Rev. J. T. Orrell. A separate group of Trustees, with their own secretary, were responsible for legal and all matters relating to the fabric of the church. When new Trust Deeds were prepared during the pastorate of Rev. Hugh Hill, the Deacons automatically became Trustees.

For many years, TCM was a member of the Baptist Union of Great Britain (BUGB), before withdrawing in 1968.[3] In the same year, TCM became affiliated to the Fellowship of Independent Evangelical Churches (FIEC).

The war years (1939–1945)

Prayer has always been, and still is, a very important part of the ministry at TCM. This was certainly true during the war years from 1939 to 1945, when TCM faced many troubles, but also experienced many blessings.

More than 50 men left TCM covered in prayer to serve in HM Forces in various parts of the world, some serving in the most dangerous campaigns. It was heart-breaking to see them

---

3   The *Minutes of the BUGB Council Meeting* (11/12 March 1969) record that '[t]he Rev. Geoffrey King had visited [TCM], as requested, and although his reception was friendly, their decision had been taken and they were not inclined to change it' (p. 62).

leave, but thanks be to God all returned safely, though, sadly, some did not return to the fellowship. However, their places were taken by men and women from various areas of the UK who were called-up to serve and stationed in camps around Lincoln. Many made TCM their spiritual home and members invited them into their own homes for times of relaxation – one in particular was known as 'Aunt Kath' (Kath Grayson), who invited countless service men and women to her home at 1 Ashlin Grove (off West Parade).

Some of those attending TCM were from other countries, including Australia, New Zealand, Canada, Jamaica, South Africa and the USA. A supper was provided for them on Sunday evenings, and thousands of meals were served during these years.

Because so many members had been called-up to serve in the forces, those remaining took on extra responsibilities in the church, as well as additional local duties. Some became Air Raid Precaution (ARP) wardens; some joined the 'Home Guard' (or 'Dad's Army'); others took on 'fire-watching' duties to protect the church building – TCM was the first place in Lincoln at which a 'fire-watching' group was formed. Although not called-up to serve in the fighting forces, those remaining at home were very much involved in the war effort and played their part in serving their king and country. One of these men was Tom Wood (Colin Wood's father), who worked at Dorman Diesels making tanks. Tom was a member of the Home Guard, and he and his wife also opened up their home to service men and women based in the area. Despite these times causing a great deal of anxiety and physical strain, there was no relaxation in prayer or the proclamation of the gospel.

Although there were many air-raids over Lincoln during the war, the night of Friday, 15 January, 1943, was particularly memorable. On this occasion there was a very heavy air-raid

Delayed-action, 2,000lb, amour-piercing, high-explosive bomb, defused by the Bomb Disposal Squad, 27 January, 1943 (picture courtesy of Lincolnshire Archives)

during which many bombs were dropped on the city. Several of these were delayed-action, high-explosive bombs which exploded one by one as time passed causing great destruction. One of these bombs fell within 30 yards of TCM and the church was rendered 'out of bounds'. After more than a week of anxious waiting, this was the only bomb that had not exploded, so on Wednesday, 27 January, the Bomb Disposal Squad began the dangerous work of rendering the bomb safe before it could be removed. It was exposed after digging down 24 feet, and after several hours the task of removing the fuse was finally completed at 7.00 pm.

A special thanksgiving meeting was held to thank God for the safety and skills of the men who undertook this work, and that in His mercy there had been no damage to the church. At the meeting a thank offering was taken up and the proceeds given to a fund for those who had suffered loss. While it was not possible to use the church during this period, joint worship services were held at Mint Street Baptist Church.

Finance

TCM has always taken a strong stand on its approach to methods of obtaining money. Because 'worldly methods' have not been used, it has been criticised over the years for being 'narrow minded'. However, this approach has glorified God, in that from the start of the work until now, every penny needed has been found without recourse to worldly methods. If a work was of God, then the church believed that He would see to it that it was not hampered through lack of funds. Specific needs have always been brought before the members, and if at times extra money was required, nothing was embarked upon unless sufficient funds were available or promised. Particularly in the early years, TCM members were not rich, but they have always been generous in their giving, not only for the needs of TCM but also to support ministries overseas. There are many instances of the ways in which God has always supplied the needs of the church; some via generous giving, others that can only be described as 'miraculous'.[4]

Local outreach – St Giles

In the 1920s, and running alongside the work at TCM, there was an outreach ministry into St Giles, quite a tough and difficult area to the north of Lincoln. The work was made doubly hard as TCM had no premises of its own in the area, and all meetings were held in a small room.

A further challenge to extend the work came in 1938, and for a number of years a large room was rented above the local branch of the Lincolnshire Co-operative store on Wragby

---

4   See *These Five and Twenty Years*, pp. 12–15, for some recorded instances.

St Giles Baptist Church Hall

St Giles Baptist Church Hall, now the Lincoln Multiple-Sclerosis Therapy Centre
(photo February 2015)

TCM members preparing the garden at St Giles
(Frank Ellis, Cec Lovely, John Yates)

Road (close to what is now the Tesco supermarket). A local resident, Mr Harold Beel, was appointed as Superintendent, ably supported by his wife Winnie, and in later years by their daughters Margaret and Vera (now Miller) and son, Derek. The work grew over the years through their faithful service, with assistance in various areas from Mr A. Chisholm, Mr A. Butt, Mr W. Dickerson, Mr C. Dean, Mr T. Wood, Mr A. Ellis and many ladies from TCM. At this time there was an afternoon Sunday School, an evening service and activities for young people during the week. Various members of TCM preached at the Sunday services.

As the work grew, plans were drawn up to build TCM's own premises. A site was purchased on Outer Circle Drive for £231 and drains laid at a cost of £146. At this point £1,050 had also been given towards the building costs, bringing the total amount contributed to over £1,400. However, because of the war years, contractors were unable to undertake the construction work, and as a result the building did not go ahead.

In the early 1950s, a large new housing estate was constructed in the north-east of the city and the Christian witness grew, particularly among the young people. The need for premises in the area was recognised and construction of the proposed building began. The structural work was carried out (and no doubt, partially financed) by a local builder Mr A. H. (Fred) Scruton, a Deacon at TCM, with much of the manual labour (digging foundations, drain trenches, etc.) provided by TCM members. Mr Jack Dixon undertook the electrical installation, and others laid out the gardens.

St Giles Baptist Church Hall opened in 1954, three years after the foundations were laid. Some 200 people celebrated God's wonderful guidance and provision as the building was dedicated and blessed at a service on Saturday, 12 June, conducted by Rev. Reginald Baker, President of the East Midlands Baptist Association.

Following the opening, various TCM members, notably Mr Jack Arden, and Mr Will Dickerson, were seconded to help run St Giles, again supported by preachers and helpers from the main church. Evangelistic missions were held, and in 1963 a part-time pastor, George Willows, was called to the work. His induction service was held on Saturday, 22 June.

Although the young people's work flourished, little impact was made among the older members of the community. Services were held each Sunday morning, taking the form of an all-age Sunday School. A Youth Club was held on Friday evenings, and a Scout troop under the leadership of Mr Beel and his son Derek ran for many years.

The work prospered for a considerable length of time under changes of leadership, but eventually, despite all the hard work, St Giles was closed and sold during 1986–7 due to dwindling numbers. Currently, the Lincoln Multiple-Sclerosis Therapy Centre is based in the premises.

The move from St Benedict's Square to High Street (1969–1972)

At the end of the 1960s, St Benedict's Square was bounded by Marks and Spencer's store and Binks Cycle Shop to the north, TCM Church to the west, the offices of the *Lincolnshire Echo* to the south, and the still-existing St Benedict's Church to the east (High Street).

At the rear of the church there was a large area of waste ground used for car parking between the Brayford Pool and the Square. The local council requisitioned this area to build a new inner relief road – now Wigford Way. This new road ran across the rear of the TCM schoolroom and kitchen, and resulted in the compulsory purchase of part of the church's land. When work started on building the road, pile-driving caused some interference in the church's activities and traffic noise increased.

Following their purchase the Binks Cycle Shop, Marks and Spencer, made an approach to the trustees of TCM to purchase the church site in order to extend their premises. The existing church was large and rambling in design, with a number of infrequently used rooms. After being in use for more than 80 years, the building was now showing signs of its age and was uneconomical to heat. There were also other problems: for example, when the baptistry, which was located

Thomas Cooper Memorial Church, St Benedict's Square, prior to demolition showing Binks Cycle Shop (photo courtesy Lincolnshire Archives)

Demolition of Thomas Cooper Memorial Church, St Benedict's Square (photo courtesy *Lincolnshire Echo*, 1972)

While demolishing the old TCM Church in St Benedict's Square, workmen found a bottle in the cavity of the foundation stone. It contained details of the stone-laying ceremony, church literature, and a copy of the *Lincoln Gazette*. The photos show Mr Bill Pullen (right) and Mr Stephen Foster, with the bottle and the front page of the newspaper (photos courtesy of *Lincolnshire Echo*)

Hannah Memorial Methodist Church, High Street, before being demolished
(photo courtesy of Lincolnshire Archives)

TCM, High Street, under construction, January 1972
(photo courtesy of Lincolnshire Archives)

TCM under construction during 1972
(photos courtesy of Lincolnshire Archives)

under the pulpit, was emptied, it leaked into the Scout den underneath it! A chance for relocation must have been very attractive to the Trustees!

The terms of the offer from Marks and Spencer were such that they would fund the construction of a new church building to the church's specification. In order to retain its witness in the city centre, TCM purchased the site of the former Hannah Memorial Methodist Church, on the corner of High Street and Chaplin Street – the location of our present church premises.

Interestingly, Binks Cycles, the church's neighbours in St Benedict's Square, also relocated to High Street, just 30 metres away, at the corner of High Street and Portland Street.

Having purchased the site of a former place of worship, no difficulty in obtaining the necessary planning permission for a new church was envisaged. The only problem foreseen was the lack of space for car parking. In order to address this, TCM purchased terraced houses in Chaplin Street as they became vacant, with a view to demolishing them in the future to provide car parking facilities.[5]

Despite proposals being submitted by a local Christian architect, the architects chosen to design the new church were Sir Frederick Gibberd and Partners, who were currently completing work on the new Roman Catholic Cathedral in Liverpool. A design was produced from a brief prepared by the Pastor, Rev. J. T. Orrell. In addition to the main church

---

5   The properties, which TCM had purchased with a view to creating a car park, were compulsorily purchased by Lincoln City Council and provided the site for the flats to the east of the building. In return, TCM was promised car parking spaces in the Council's Chaplin Street car park, and a drawing was produced indicating a parking layout. However, over the passing of time, the Council could find no record of this agreement, and TCM's Title Deeds confirming the agreement, had also disappeared, which resulted in a new set of Title Deeds being prepared in the early part of 2000.

building, the design included a number of small rooms to the rear to house Sunday School classes. With a view to minimising the potential risk of vandalism, high-level windows to all parts of the premises featured prominently in the design.

Tender documents and a full specification[6] were prepared, and the contract was awarded to the newly-formed building contractors, Pelham Construction. This company was created by two former directors of a well-known Lincoln building company, Frank R. Eccleshare (Mayor and founder of LACE housing for older people), Roy Dowson, a Christian, and his colleague, Alan Walker. Around the same time, they also won a contract to build Homer House in Monson Street, to form the offices of Godfrey Holmes Ltd, which is built in similar brickwork to that used for TCM.

When work commenced on the site, several members of TCM were involved in the construction. Colin Davies, father of Ruth Wood, was appointed Clerk of Works; Steve Holman of Thornton-Firkin and Partners acted as Quantity Surveyor; Michael Wilson and John Cotton were employed by Pelham Construction. The electrical work was undertaken by R. Daubney & Co. Ltd, and Martin Daubney supervised the installation. Electric underfloor heating was installed to heat the main areas of the building, which at that time was quite a new concept.

The ground conditions were found to be quite poor, and a system called vibro-compaction was used to stabilise the substructure, which involved vibrating and compacting gravel piers in the ground. This resulted in beer glasses falling off the racks in the Blue Anchor public house across the road, with a subsequent claim for compensation!

Although the budget for the new premises appeared to be

---

6   The specification is available in TCM's archived documents.

Opening of TCM, High Street, 9 September, 1972

Opening of TCM High Street, 9 September, 1972
(photo courtesy of Lincolnshire Archives)

Platform party at the opening of TCM, 9 September 1972
(*left to right*): Rev. J. T. Orrell, Rev. A. G. Morton; Rev. J. Shelbourne, Mr J. Salt,
Mr D. R. Dowson, Rev. F. H. Inger; (*centre*): Dr Martyn Lloyd-Jones (*guest speaker*)

adequate, certain savings had to be made. One of these was the omission of plaster to the main church building, resulting in the painted brickwork which is still visible. This prompted the comment by Bobby Ball, the comedian, during an evangelistic meeting that, 'It will look good when it's finished!'

Also, it transpired that there was insufficient money available to furnish and fit-out the building properly. So, a deputation, led by Deacon A. H. (Fred) Scruton, visited Marks and Spencer in London with a request for additional funding, which fortunately was provided.

Some artefacts were salvaged from the old church and refixed in the new building, including the plaques on the rear wall, and the original masonry name stone was built into a wall specially erected on the north boundary of the new site.

While demolishing the old TCM building in St Benedict's Square, workmen found a bottle in the cavity of the foundation stone, which contained details of the stone-laying ceremony, church literature, and a copy of the *Lincoln Gazette* newspaper (see photos on p. 109).

The final design was described by Nikolaus Pevsner in his book *Lincolnshire (Pevsner Architectural Guides: Buildings of England)* as 'an effective image, bold but austere'.

The opening ceremony was held on Saturday, 9 September, 1972, with the speaker being the late eminent preacher and author Dr Martyn Lloyd-Jones from Westminster Chapel. Despite it being a very warm day, the 'Doctor' preached in his overcoat!

The platform party included the Pastor, Rev. J. T. Orrell, Rev. John Shelbourne of the New Life Church, Lincoln, and the President of the East Midlands Baptist Union. The church was full to capacity, with a thirty-voice choir, local dignitaries, and the project architects, George Dunton and Peter Fleig.

Mission, past and present

TCM has always supported missionary societies working in various parts of the world and the United Kingdom through prayer and financial giving, and there have also been those who have been called by God to serve Him overseas. We now mention some of the TCM members called to this work over the years and the missions currently supported by TCM.

Past mission

Miss Jean Chisholm – Morocco

After spending two years at the Bible Training Institute in Glasgow, Jean Chisholm went to Morocco in November, 1927, to work with the Southern Morocco Mission. Initally, Jean was stationed at Marrakesh, then, after learning the language, moved to a new station at Amismiz at the foot of the Atlas mountains to reach out to the Berbers, a tribe of wild hillmen.

She served the Lord in that needy region until 1939, when because of ill-health she was invalided home, but continued to pray for and support the work of the mission. Jean went to be with the Lord on 3 April, 1993.

Miss Annie Bayram – Nigeria (see also Appendix 4)
Annie Bayram was converted at TCM, and after serving the church for several years, particularly assisting with the Cubs, went to study at Mount Hermon Bible College. She had 'a very capable knowledge of medicine . . . spent a year at Lincoln County Hospital and was for a time a dispenser at the chemist shop of Mr J. Hague, of Lincoln.'[7] In 1933, TCM helped finance her move to Nigeria to work with the Sudan Interior Mission (SIM). While learning the lanaguage, she was based at Minna, then posted to the Gbari town of Paiko. After twenty-eight years as a missionary, she died in Nigeria in 1961.

Mr Norman Hunter – Nigeria
Norman Hunter was a businessman who had been converted and a member of TCM. In 1938, an earnest desire to become a missionary, together with his business skills, resulted in him accepting an important post on the staff of the Sudan Interior Mission (SIM) to manage their bookshop in Jos, Nigeria. He soon recognised a pressing need to share the gospel with the natives in the nearby town of Yelwa, which he undertook once the shop had closed on Saturday mornings. After gaining their confidence, Norman was instrumental in establishing a flour-ishing church. He also travelled extensively in Nigeria looking for opportunities to extend the work, and produced films which were shown in the UK and the USA to promote the work of SIM. He later served with the British and Foreign

---

7   Newspaper article, 9 June 1961.

Bible Society and worked with the United Bible Society of South Africa.

Philip and Mary Osbourne

Philip Osbourne was from Washingborough, and a former pupil of Lincoln Christ's Hospital School. Mary was an American. They served together with SIM in the bookshop in Jos, Nigeria, supported by TCM and Mary's church in Maryland, USA. Prayer meetings were held on a regular basis at Philip's parents' home in Washingborough. On their retirement they went to live in Maryland, but continued to visit the UK and TCM, particularly for the Keswick Convention and other missionary events.

Miss Edna Hutchins – Bengal, Burma and the USA

After serving at TCM for several years, Edna Hutchins went to be a nurse companion to an invalid in Alnwick, Northumberland. While there she helped in the local chapel and was responsible for the conversion of many young people. This prepared her for God's call on her life, when in 1939 an opportunity came that she had been praying for – to go as a missionary helper in the St Andrew's Homes and Hospital in the Kalimpong Hills, Bengal, run by the Church of Scotland. When war broke out, the situation in India became difficult and after Japan's attack on Burma in 1942, evacuation of the children in the mission was begun. However, Edna went into Burma with other missionaries to work with the British and American Red Cross caring for the sick and wounded. Conditions were appalling, and daily they were being pushed back until they found themselves stranded in India, with little hope of evacuation. By the grace of God, a place was found for Edna on an American ship and she eventually arrived in the USA with no earthly possessions. Still wanting to serve the Lord, she took a position as a wardress in a women's penitentiary for coloured people. Despite the horrendous conditions, Edna shared the gospel with these outcast criminals, and through her perseverance and prayer several women were converted. Her section was also the best behaved in the penitentiary.

Miss Mary Stimpson – Nigeria

In June 1939, Mary Stimpson, a member of TCM, went to Nigeria, after working as a nurse for seven years and as a student at Mount Hermon Bible College. As a fully qualified State Registered Nurse and midwife she served on the staff of the Sudan Interior Mission (SIM) in Jos, supervising the maternity work, and as a nurse and dispenser at the Mission hospital.

Miss Gladys Reader – Nigeria

After completing her training and qualifying as a State Registered Nurse and midwife, Gladys (Jane) Reader spent two years at the Mount Hermon Bible College before going to Nigeria in 1944 to join other TCM members on the staff of the Sudan Interior Mission (SIM). Once she had learnt the language at Minna she was allocated to a missionary station. Later, she returned home to nurse her aged mother, and, incidentally, was Steve Holman's godmother.

Mr Bob Hodson – SASRA

Bob became a member of SASRA prior to two years' National Service in the Army, after which he left the Army and went to Bible college in Berwick-on-Tweed. With the agreement of SASRA and the Commanding Officer of the King's Own Scottish Borderers, he became a part-time Scripture Reader, expecting to be able to become a full-time Reader at the end of the project. However, having served for only two years in the Army and not attained a senior non-commissioned rank, he was not eligible for the appointment, and returned home to Lincoln, where he was appointed as a part-time Scripture Reader to the two Army barracks in the city and the Nocton Hall RAF Hospital.

In 1958 Bob became a full-time Scripture Reader and in 1959 was sent to Aden. He travelled on a troop ship and had access to the whole ship, giving him many opportunities to share the gospel with all the ranks on board. While in Aden, Bob visited service personnel in the Army and the RAF, and had opportunities to give *Thought for the Day* on Radio Aden. It was here that he met his wife, Barbara, a nursing sister with the Queen Elizabeth's Overseas Nursing Service, and they were married on 1 July, 1961. Ten days after their marriage, Bob and Barbara found themselves on a troop ship passing through Aden en route to Hong Kong.

In Hong Kong, Bob had many opportunities to share the gospel during meetings with men on the bases and visits to hospitals, as well as with men in a detention centre on the island of Lantau. In 1962, Bob moved to Singapore to continue his work with SASRA. Some of those he shared the gospel with became Christians and went to the mission field or other areas of Christian service. Bob and Barbara's elder daughter, Priscilla, was born in Singapore prior to returning to the UK in 1966.

Back in the UK, Bob was sent to the Salisbury Plain and served there for three years. During this period the couple's younger daughter, Miriam, was born. The next move, in 1969, was to the Münster and Osnabrück areas in Germany, before returning to the UK in 1976 to work in RAF stations in Lincolnshire. Further moves followed: Germany in 1979 to Celle, working in the Lüneburg Heath training area and the military hospital in Hannover; UK in 1985, working on three RAF stations – North Luffenham, Wittering and Cottesmore; Germany in 1988 to Bergen-Belsen, again working in the

Lüneburg Heath area. During this period Bob and Barbara were invited to a service held in The Guards Chapel, Wellington Barracks, London, celebrating 150 years of SASRA's work since its foundation. HM the Queen, the Patron of SASRA, attended the service, and along with others they were presented to the Queen at a reception afterwards.

Approaching retirement, in 1993 Bob and Barbara returned to the UK and again worked on the three RAF stations in the Rutland area, where there were many opportunities to share the gospel. Just before retiring, RAF North Luffenham closed, but Bob volunteered to remain working as a part-time Scripture Reader covering the other two stations. However, this ended abruptly in the early autumn of 1998, when Bob suffered an attack, thought to be epilepsy, and had to surrender his driving licence. At the beginning of 1999 Bob suffered another attack, but after a year without further attacks his driving licence was returned. Now retired, Bob and Barbara currently live in Lincoln and continue to worship regularly at TCM, where their contribution as members is greatly valued and appreciated.

Dr Ian and Mrs Audrey Sharpe – Congo

Ian and Audrey Sharpe (née Gibson) were missionaries from TCM serving with the Unevangelised Fields Mission in the Congo. As a girl, Audrey was a member of the Sunday School and the Girl Guides, and baptised at TCM. She then became a nurse, and met her husband, Ian, while she was training. They were married at TCM. Ian was a doctor, and performed many difficult operations successfully in primitive conditions in the Congo. Audrey's parents and her sister, Margaret, were TCM members, who lived on the Ermine estate. In 1964, Ian and Audrey were caught up in the Simba uprising, and together with their three children, Jillian (8), Alison (7) and Andrew (4) were martyred. Their bodies were never recovered, although torn and bloodstained clothing and papers identified as belonging to them were discovered at Banalia. A memorial plaque can be found in the main body of the church on the rear wall. (See also Appendix 4.)

Miss Berenice Ducker – SASRA

Having served in the RAF Police from 1990–1993, Berenice attended the University of Wales, Bangor, where she became a Christian in 1997. In 2001, she was called by God to work with the military through the Soldiers' and Airmen's Scripture Readers Association (SASRA), and began working with the organisation in 2002. After training, Berenice was posted to Lincolnshire RAF bases, where she served from 2003–2011, living at RAF Digby and visiting RAF bases at Waddington, Coningsby, Cranwell, and later Cottesmore and Wittering in the Rutland area. During this time she attended TCM, and became a member of the church. With God's help, Berenice took the gospel to servicemen and supported Christians serving in the military; predominately RAF personnel, although there were also Navy and Army personnel on the bases. Initially, she made brief visits to section tea bars and squadron crew rooms to introduce herself and get to know people. Eventually, she ran tea bars for a week at a time in order to spend more time with personnel, hoping for opportunities to share the gospel as well as caring for those she visited. Although it took almost five years before she felt accepted on the bases, she was able to give out literature and had many discussions on the Christian faith, as well as experiencing the joy of seeing an Army officer come to faith in Christ.

Oradea, Romania

In the late 1990s, an association was formed with a Baptist church in Oradea, Romania, and in particular their Pastor, Emil

Bartos. A trust was set up (jointly managed by Mally Dolby, [née Daubney]) to sponsor students through Bible College in Oradea, where Emil was also a lecturer. Mally and another trustee used to visit each year to check on the students, and parcels of clothing etc. were taken, as the church members and students were extremely poor. At this time, church services were being held in a converted bakery which was full to overflowing. On one occasion, those visiting from TCM were asked for advice about a new church building which was being planned. Subsequently, TCM supported the work financially, and the church, a magnificent circular structure, was built.

Others
Although details over time have become sketchy, there are others whose names should be mentioned.

Ann Sanders – The *TCM Monthly Magazine* for February 1965 records that Ann had 'settled in to work among the "Life Brigade"'. However, there are no further details supplied.

Gillian Cockfield – Gillian served with the Overseas Missionary Fellowship (OMF), and was commissioned at a service at TCM in January, 1974.

Ian Dixon – Ian was the son of the then Church Secretary, George Dixon. He went to Bible college and then was a pastor in Strabane, Northern Ireland, at height of the Irish troubles. Subsequently, he moved to Canada and pastored Trinity Baptist Church, Hamilton, Ontario. He married Evelyn and had two sons. At the time of writing, his sister, Ann Milner, lives on Burton Road, Lincoln.

Rosemary Gourlay – Rosemary, a former teacher at Lincoln Girls High school, went as a missionary to France at La Charité-sur-Loire (twinned with Branston).

Mary Grundy – Mary spent several years as a nurse at Lincoln County Hospital, then as a midwife at hospitals in London,

Leeds and Watford, as well as a year at the Mildway Mission Hospital, before going to serve with the Red Sea Mission in the Aden Protectorate in 1962.

Joan Nicholson – Middle East Christian Outreach, Lebanon.

Graham and Pauline Wiggett – Graham and Pauline went to serve with SIM in Niger.

Susan Howarth – At the time of writing, Susan is retired, after serving for many years with New Tribes Mission (NTM) in Guinea, directly supporting the efforts of Bible translators and missionaries by teaching children.

Present mission (at the time of writing)
Azarja and Renee Groot – Mercy Air, South Africa

Azarja and Renee became members of TCM during their year-long training course at New Tribes Mission (NTM) in 2008. They were fully involved in church life and celebrated the arrival of their first child, Elliora. Azarja's parents were missionaries who established several churches in Ivory Coast before becoming representatives for the Netherlands branch of NTM. Renee was also the child of missionary parents and she met Azarja when they went to university. Upon successful completion of their studies the couple were married. When the Groots had completed their training at NTM, they returned to the USA. Azarja continued to develop his aircraft mechanic and piloting skills while waiting on the Lord for direction as to where they should serve. During this period they embarked on some 'church growth' and were blessed by the arrival of baby Esther. Since August 2012 the Groots have been serving with Mercy Air in South Africa. In 2014 they received a further blessing with the arrival of their son Ezra.

Graham Herbert – Eurasian Ministries

Graham serves as the interim director for Eurasian Ministries

UK, which supports the work of the Eurasian College. This college is located within the Russian Federation, in the city of Kazan, Taterstan. Established in 1999, the college runs a full-time residential missionary training programme. Students complete a year of full-time study then spend another year being supervised in the field, normally somewhere in central Asia. The college also runs a continuing education programme to maintain support to their graduates throughout their ministries. This part of the world has a majority muslim population and persecution is commonplace. The vision of the Eurasian College is to raise up successive generations of missionaries from the mission-minded churches they establish, train them and send them as skilled gospel preachers and pastors to reach some of the least evangelised peoples of the world. Graham's duties include; sharing the colleges needs and news, raising support as well as frequently travelling to lecture at the college.

Allan and Lorraine Knowles – African Leadership

Allan and Lorraine Knowles serve with African Leadership based in Cape Town, South Africa. Their ministry works with the poor and disadvantaged, whose poverty and lack of qualifications would otherwise prevent them from entering formal biblical training. African Leadership aims to produce Bible-centred leaders to serve locally as labourers harvesting in the fields of the Great Commission. Students study part time over two years, for more than 400 hours. Allan is normally able to visit TCM once a year as part of his fund and awareness raising travels.

Sean and Sylvia Marcus – TULCA Foundation, Romania

After visiting Romania, Sean and Sylvia Marcus were so affected by the needs of the community that they sold up and relocated to Tulca. They established the TULCA Foundation where they currently serve – a ministry that involves expressing God's love for the poor and marginalised in society. In practice, this means meeting the basic educational and health needs of a number of Roma children who would otherwise be rejected or exploited by the society in which they live.

Will McKinney – USA
Will was a member at TCM during his two-year stint as the United States Naval officer on exchange to RAF Waddington. Following his return to the USA, Will completed his full-time service and commenced studies at the Trinity International University seminary college in Chicago, Illinois. Will has maintained a partnership with a church community in the Ukraine which he visited several times in order to share the gospel through preaching and other practical support. Following his marriage in 2015, Will is seeking the Lord's leading for his area of service when his studies are complete.

Isaac and Gloria Shaw – Delhi Bible Institute (DBI)
Isaac and Gloria serve with the Delhi Bible Institute which has a vision to reach the people of Northern India. Specifically, DBI plans to train 30,000 students, plant 15,000 Bible-preaching churches and establish twelve regional training centres by 2025. Since 2008 TCM has been in partnership with Isaac who serves as the executive director of DBI where he has been on the staff for almost thirty years. In 2011 Rev. Mike Smailes was able to travel to India and augment the teaching staff for two weeks.

Hannah Jackson
In August 2012, Hannah left TCM to spend a year working with the Africa Inland Mission (AIM), in Korr, a remote desert part of northern Kenya, where she taught Rendille children

at Tirrim Secondary School. *Tirrim* is the Rendille word for 'cornerstone' because Christ is at the centre of the work. Currently, the Tirrim Project also runs nursery schools in traditional villages and three primary schools. Between them they educate and feed more than 1,000 Rendille children who would otherwise be destitute and uneducated. Hannah worked alongside an amazing couple who had been working with the Rendille tribe in Korr for over 30 years, transcribing their language for the first time and translating the Bible, as well as establishing Christian adult education classes and a veterinary evangelism scheme. Hannah returned to the UK and TCM in August 2013.

Christian Concern for Our Nation (CCFON)

CCFON have a passion to see the UK return to the Christian faith and is supported by TCM. In the last few decades our nation has largely turned its back on Jesus. The fruit of this can be seen in widespread family breakdown, immorality and social disintegration. Yet hope can be found in Jesus Christ. CCFON seek to awaken the Church, become a light and a witness to the nation, and are passionate about their faith. Futher details can be found at www.christianconcern.com.

Good News Broadcasting (GNB)

TCM has had an interest in and supported Good News Broadcasting since the late 1980s, following a visit from the then director, David Oram, when GNB was based at Bawtry. (In January 2006, GNB relocated to purpose-built premises in Ranskill.) At time of the visit, Rev. McClatchey was the Pastor, and shortly afterwards he and Colin Wood were invited onto the Board of Trustees. Rev. McClatchey resigned from the Board when he left TCM, but Colin remained a Trustee until he retired after serving for 13 years. The work has also been supported by several members of TCM who travelled to GNB to broadcast, notably Rev. Hugh Hill, who gave a number of talks. Currently, Mark Williams, one of the deacons, is the Media Director at GNB, continuing TCM's interest and support for the work of spreading the gospel over the airwaves. Further details about GNB can be found at www.gnba.net.

Music and local outreach

Music has always played a very large part in the ministry of TCM. Mr Radford was extremely musical and formed a choir, which led the morning and evening worship every week, and sang an item during each evening service. During the winter months, 'Song Services' were held following the evening service, and once a month 'fishers' went out into the streets of Lincoln to invite folk in for refreshments and to hear the gospel in song and word. Members of the choir were encouraged to give their testimonies at these informal gatherings, and the schoolroom at the back of the church was usually full. During the war, and until National Service ended in the early 1960s, the surrounding area of Lincoln had many RAF stations and army camps and the servicemen and women were only too glad to come to TCM on a Sunday evening. Many were converted as a result of being presented with the gospel. After Mr Radford's retirement, others took hold of the baton, and the choir remained an important part of worship and gospel outreach. The choir also sang during visits to small village chapels, hospitals, institutions and prisons in the surrounding areas.

During the 1960s, teams led by Mr Will Dickerson went to St George's Hospital on Thursday evenings and the County Hospital on Sunday afternoons to hold services. These were discontinued when the NHS required a multi-faith approach.

A male voice choir was also formed, and on several occasions sang at the Royal Albert Hall in London at the Festival of Male Voice Praise, one year singing with over 1,000 male voices from all over the United Kingdom. Colin Wood conducted practices in Lincoln followed by final rehearsals in the Royal Albert Hall before singing to the public in the evening. Colin's father, Tom, organised coach trips to the event for several years, which included some sightseeing in London beforehand.

While TCM was located in St Benedict's Square, a two-manual pipe organ was mainly used to accompany the singing, supplemented with piano and other orchestral intruments on occasion. During the early days of the Mission, the organ was played by Mr F. Martin with assistance from Mr J. Blake, Mr J. Lingard and Mr W. Froggatt, but for the majority of the time when Mr Cecil H. Radford was the Honorary Pastor it was played by his wife, Mrs Elsie Radford.

The pipe organ was not moved during the relocation to High Street. A Hammond organ and a grand piano were used to accompany the singing for a number of years, but an electronic keyboard, guitars, drums and other instruments were introduced when TCM adopted a more contemporary style of worship.

Youth work

Youth work, too, has always been a significant part of TCM's ministry. During the early years there were more than three hundred children in two Sunday Schools, one in the morning and one in the afternoon. In addition there was another large meeting held on Tuesday evenings. This ministry was under the leadership of Mr Arthur Wilson, supported by many devoted workers. His faithful service over many years was acknowledged first in 1931, when he was honoured by having the presidency of the Lincoln Sunday School Union conferred upon him, and then in January, 1943, when he was presented with a monetary gift and a scroll commemorating fifty-five years of service to the church.

The children attending these meetings were drawn mostly from the area immediately surrounding St Benedict's Square. At the time, the quality of houses in this area was very poor, resulting in them being condemned and the occupants moving to new housing in the suburbs of Lincoln. Over 200 children moved, which significantly reduced Sunday School numbers. Following intensive house-to-house visitations some new children began attending, which together with an increase in the number of TCM members' children compensated to some extent for the reduction in numbers.

New and more interesting methods of teaching Bible knowledge were then introduced on Sunday afternoons. The name was changed from 'Sunday School' to 'Radiant Hour', and the scholars were called 'Radiants'. A 'Teens' section with a 'spiritual core' known as the 'Inner Circle' was also established in 1946, led initially by Mr Peter Radford. Some of the so-called 'Teens' were subsequently baptised, became members of TCM and served the church in various ways. Others moved away from the area, but many can testify that the grounding they received during their early years at TCM equipped them to face the challenges presented by the world.

The uniformed organisations, Scouts, Guides, Cubs and Brownies also ran successfully for many years, mainly run by the following Christian leaders, although others, not mentioned here, gave valuable assistance:

- **Scouts (22nd Lincoln):** *Group Scoutmasters* – Cecil H. Radford, succeeded by Jack Wood; *Leaders* – Jack Wood, succeeded by Eric Oxby, assisted by Steve Holman

- **Girl Guides (16th Lincoln):** Elsie Radford, Elsie Yates, succeeded by Linda Oxby, assisted by Jacqui Holman
- **Wolf Cubs (22nd Lincoln):** Tom Holman, assisted by Madge Carline, Molly Peadon and Mary Osbourne, succeeded by Chris Osbourne, assisted by Arnold Davill
- **Brownies (16th Lincoln):** Phyllis Purdue, succeeded by Margaret Davill

After nearly more than sixty years, the decision was taken in 1987 to discontinue the Scouts, Guides and Cubs at TCM, following the introduction of a multi-faith approach and changes to the Scout and Guide Promises (the Brownies continued to run for several more years). During this period, thirty-three Guides attained their Queen's Guide award. When a Venture Scout Troop (now Explorer Scouts) was started by Eric Oxby, two members of the Troop qualified as Queen's Scouts and travelled to Windsor Castle to receive their awards.

Youth work has continued to flourish, although over the years it has been adapted to meet members' and changing demographic needs. At the time of writing, the ministry to young people has been developed over the last few years under the leadership of Mrs Rowena Kirkby, supported by TCM members and students attending TCM while studying in Lincoln. The current ministry extends to young parents with babies, children and young people up to the age of eighteen, and includes outreach into local schools working alongside the Joy Foundation.[8]

---

8 The Joy Foundation is a Lincolnshire based charity working in the local community, supported by local churches and organisations, promoting education, life skills and the Christian faith through word and deed, both in schools and the wider community. See www.joyfoundation.org.uk.

Current student ministry

Following the opening of the University of Lincoln in 1996 and the former Bishop Grosseteste teacher training college being granted full university status in 2012, the number of students in Lincoln has increased significantly. As a result of the ministry to students begun by Richard Wardman and continued by others, TCM has developed strong links with the Christian Unions at both institutions, and assists with CU missions and outreach. Over recent years a growing number of students have attended TCM – some already Christians, wishing to continue worshipping and serving the Lord after moving from their home churches; others becoming Christians while studying in Lincoln.

TCM currently provides ministry to students under the umbrella name of *Ignition*, led by Joel and Hannah Murray (former students who met at the CU). *Ignition* includes a variety of activities during term time, with the central aims of discipling students who will give their lives wholly to Jesus Christ to be used by Him, and preparing them for life after university. Students are encouraged to become actively involved in the life and ministries of the church; typically, helping with the Music Team, Children's and Youth Work, PA and Visuals, Welcome Team, Welcome Café or the Library.

After leaving university, some students have found employment locally and currently remain serving the Lord at TCM, while others, following a period at TCM, have subsequently moved away.

The future . . .

Since the resignation of Rev. Mike Smailes in 2013, TCM has been faithfully led to date (May 2015) by the current eldership

– Martin Daubney, Ian Kirkby and Rodger Moomba – assisted by the deacons, ministry team leaders and other TCM members. During this period, the former Pastor, Rev. Hugh Hill, Andrew Miller, guests, and members of the church have maintained the preaching of God's Word on Sundays.

As this book goes to press, God has graciously answered the prayers of the church for a new Pastor. The Rev. Maurice Kinnaird has accepted the call to become the next Pastor to continue leading the ministry and witness of TCM in proclaiming the gospel of the Lord Jesus Christ.

Before entering the pastoral ministry, Maurice engaged in full-time evangelism in the UK for five years (1978–1983). After studying in London Theological Seminary for two years (1983–1985), his first pastorate was in Crowfield Grace Baptist Church, Suffolk, which lasted for five years. He and his family then moved to the Wirral, where Maurice was the Pastor of Hoylake Evangelical Church. Since 2002, he has been the Senior Pastor at Ebenezer Baptist Church in Mold, Flintshire. Maurice and his wife, Lynda, have been married for 33 years, and they have four grown-up sons.

A new chapter is about to begin . . .

Appendix 1

Thomas Cooper (1805–1892)

 Thomas Cooper was born in Leicester on 20 March, 1805, at the time of the Napoleonic Wars. In this country, desperate Luddite workers were destroying the machines which were forcing many of them out of work and towards starvation.

Thomas's father died when he was only four years old, and his widowed mother returned to her home town of Gainsborough, Lincolnshire, where Thomas subsequently grew up. He experienced poverty during his early years – sometimes there were only potatoes to eat. His mother struggled to have him educated, despite Thomas working when possible to provide additional income.

Aged fifteen, he ran away to sea, but after serving for only nine days, the brutality of the life sickened him and, surprisingly, he was released. After returning home he worked thirteen-hour days as a shoemaker, but still found time to educate himself in Greek, Latin, Hebrew, French and algebra. He learnt seven Shakespeare plays by heart, and the first three books of *Paradise Lost*. In order to do so, he rose at 3 or 4am to study, then worked until 8 or 9pm – an astonishing programme of self-education, which inevitably led to him having a complete physical and emotional breakdown.

In 1827 Cooper gave up cobbling to become a schoolmaster, and later, a Methodist preacher. His affairs did not prosper, and after going to Lincoln, where he obtained work on a local newspaper, he went to London in 1839, taking a post as an assistant to a second-hand bookseller. In November, 1840, he began work with the *Leicestershire Mercury*. Deeply moved by the poverty he saw in Leicester, he became a Chartist.[1] Cooper believed strongly that all men deserved the vote, and started leading meetings, which he began with a prayer. One of his themes was that the poor, down-trodden masses were, 'just as Jesus was, persecuted by bad men and wicked laws!' He also wrote Chartist hymns.

Cooper's energy and ability as a public speaker enabled him to become a great leader of the Chartist cause and one impassioned speech led him to disaster. After the strikes in the Potteries in 1842, he was arrested and tried for 'seditious conspiracy' and imprisoned for two years in Stafford jail, a foul Victorian prison. At the time, his wife Susanna was close to death, and under the circumstances, he turned from God. While in prison, he wrote his most famous work, *The Purgatory of Suicides*.

Following his release in 1845, he embarked on his great mission: to educate the working man. As he was well known and a fiery a speaker, he drew the crowds, lecturing on history, literature and science. Although at first he spoke against religion, he never doubted the beauty of Christ's character.

In 1856, with a lecture booked, he found himself physically and mentally unable to speak on his chosen subject. He renounced the free-thinking doctrines which he had held for many years, and became a lecturer on Christian evidences.

---

1 Chartism was a working class movement, which emerged in 1836 and was most active between 1838 and 1848. The aim of the Chartists was to gain political rights and influence for the working classes. Chartism got its name from the formal petition, or People's Charter, that listed the six main aims of the movement.

From then on, God was his subject matter – Thomas Cooper had returned to Christianity!

Life remained a struggle. Both he and his wife suffered ill health, and his wife died in February, 1880, aged 78. Despite this, his miraculous survival of a train crash assured him of God's hand on his life.

With his life recommitted to Christ, Cooper spent many years travelling across Britain delivering lectures and sermons, preaching against Darwinism and delivering a simple Christian message.

In the 1870s he settled in Lincoln, and in 1876 Thomas Cooper became a member of the General Baptist Church in Lincoln. Subsequently, he frequently preached there to crowded congregations and attended the church until his death on 15 July,1892, aged 87. He was buried with his wife Susanna and her sister Letitia; their grave is in the Canwick Road Old Cemetery, Lincoln. At the time of his death he had few possessions – any money he was given, he gave away.

As a fitting memorial to Thomas Cooper – shoemaker, teacher, journalist, revolutionary political activist, convict, poet, author . . . then called by God to be an evangelist and preacher based in Lincoln – the Annual General Church Meeting of the General Baptist Church held on 1 January, 1884, unanimously agreed that, when erected, the new church building should be called the Thomas Cooper Memorial Church. Thomas Cooper gave his consent to the proposal; hence the name of the current church – reflecting the text 'persecuted, but not abandoned' (2 Corinthians 4:9).

Appendix 2

Cecil H. Radford, Honorary Pastor of TCM – thirty-five years of ministry from 1924–1958

In 1907, two boys from the Sunday School at the General Baptist Church in Lincoln attended an evangelistic meeting in Derby led by Rev. Philip Hudgell. At the end of the meeting there was an appeal to receive Christ, and these two timid boys raised their hands in response. One of these boys was eight-year-old Cecil Radford; the other was ten-year-old Donald Miller. Little did they realise at the time the significance of their decisions, or what plans God had for their lives.

After growing up they went their separate ways, although both served in the First World War, both went into business, and both were called by God into fuller service for Him. Donald Miller went to India working among the lepers, eventually becoming the Secretary for India of the Mission to Lepers. Cecil Radford remained in Lincoln, became a preacher and led the spiritual side of the work at the Kirke White Club for Youths and Boys, before returning as Honorary Pastor of TCM Memorial Church, where in his early years he had been baptised and become a member of the church.

Years later, while on a trip home from India, Donald Miller visited TCM where Cecil Radford was now the Pastor – a happy reunion followed. At the time, Rev. Philip Hudgell was in Bognor Regis and through a series of 'coincidences' heard the story, and another reunion was arranged at TCM – it was a memorable occasion! Rev. Hudgell said, 'I thought that mission had been a failure. I went back home greatly dispirited – what little faith I had. After many days God has spared my life to see the fruit of that week's mission.'

In front of a packed church on Sunday morning, 2 March, 1924, Cecil Radford married Miss Elsie M. Hodgson, whose supreme unselfishness enabled her husband to fulfil his responsibilites as Pastor. For the rest of her life she devoted herself to serving the Lord in many ways at TCM, not least as organist and Captain of the Girl Guides.

In 1934, in recognition of years of selfless and undgrudging voluntary services from Cecil Radford and his wife, the TCM membership and children contributed a sufficient amount of money to purchase a Standard 9 saloon car and prepare illuminated addresses for each of them. The presentation was

The Standard 9 car presented to Mr and Mrs Radford

138

made on 21 February in a packed church with leading citizens, representatives from city churches and other organisations in attendance.

After completing twenty-one years' service, further appreciation in the form of monetary gifts (because of the war years) was made to each of them.

After twenty-five years' service a TCM member wrote the following as a tribute to him, 'the deacons having expressed their hearty agreement with the sentiments contained therein':

> This would not be a complete account of TCM and its people without a word about the man, who under the good hand of God, has been behind all these activities. I count it an honour to be allowed, on behalf of all the members of TCM, to add to this Souvenir, a tribute to our beloved Pastor, Mr Cecil H. Radford.
>
> Some of us remember him as he came in those very early days, a young man, very slim and frail, yet giving the impression of unbounded energy and drive, only held in check by physical weakness. His doctor gave him six months to live if he insisted on taking over the care of the Church. This young man had a vision. Lying on his back for twelve hours each day during the five years after leaving the Forces, he had had time to dream and read. God knew what was best, for in those five years this young man had learned much. He accepted those years as a time of preparation, and dreamed of the time when God should call him. His Bible and his Bible books were his companions. When the call came in 1923 he was equipped and ready.
>
> Possessing a most attractive personality, and endowed far above the average with natural gifts, he has used his talents unstintingly for His Lord and this Church, and God has been pleased to bless his ministry to the salvation of hundreds of souls. His persuasive powers and driving force have carried the

Church to great endeavours, and thousands will live to thank God that they ever came into touch with him. He has not only been the 'man in the pulpit', but has ever been willing to help with the more humble jobs, and beginners in all departments have found him ready with help, advice and unlimited encouragement.

He is a most able teacher as well as a preacher, and is acceptable to old and young alike. Perhaps the greatest tribute we can pay to him as a preacher, is to say that his ministry is as fresh and powerful today as it was twenty-five years ago.

He never does things by halves, but puts his whole soul into his work, and has taught us by example, that nothing less than our best should be offered in service to our Master.

He has rarely taken a day off, and time spent on holiday during the whole of his pastorate does not amount to eight weeks. On enquiry, we discovered that he has preached and lectured nearly 4,000 times and given 1,250 children's addresses, in addition to innumerable short talks. He has conducted over 12,000 meetings.

His work amongst the children and young people has always been with marked success. They love him. He is a great disciplinarian, and can be friendly with the most unruly crowd of children, without losing dignity or his control over the meeting.

Not only as a speaker, but as a musician and singer of no mean ability, his work will never be forgotten.

As a shrewd business man, his guidance on all financial matters has been of untold benefit to the Church and has saved us hundreds of pounds. Speaking of him as a business man, we would like to put it on record that in all these years he has never allowed his Church work to suffer through the daily work done for his firm. He has done two men's work and done it well. Some of us know a little about the 'midnight oil' which he has burned in order that both jobs might be accomplished. As a partner, and later as Managing Director of his Company, he has had sufficient responsibility to occupy his whole time, but to that he has added the full time work of Pastor of this Church. We honour him for it. His money, his time and his talents have been poured out in one long stream, and we rejoice with him that God has enabled him to do a work which will live for ever in the annals of the Church.

We shall ever hold him in high esteem for his own sake and for his work's sake. Nay, more than that, we shall always love him, for we cannot think of TCM without our beloved Pastor.

Cecil Radford continued to pastor TCM faithfully until his retirement in 1958. In the words of his family, Cecil Radford 'entered the Homeland 4th April, 1959, aged 60 years', and is buried in the Newport Cemetery, Lincoln.

To commemorate his thirty-five years of faithful service, a memorial plaque was unveiled by his lifetime friend, Donald Miller, at a special service conducted by Rev. Harry Whyte and attended by many old friends on Saturday, 18 November, 1961.

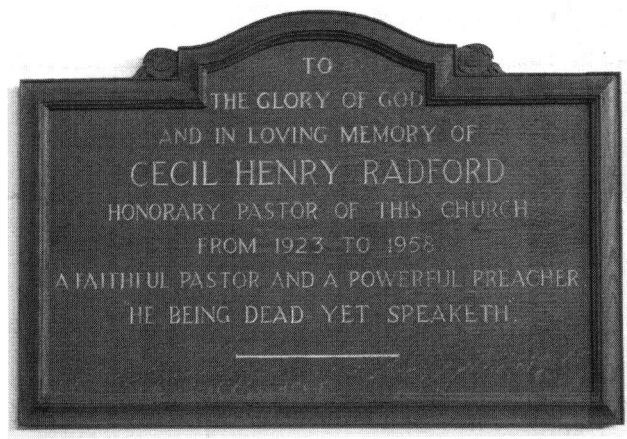

Appendix 3

Appendix 3 lists all those who from the early days have had the responsibility of preaching, leading or pastoring TCM at St Benedict's Square and High Street. Cross-references are provided to locations in the text where further information or biographical details can be found.

Name	Dates
Early preachers	
Mr William Paine (see p. 53)	c. 1660–?
Mr Roger Fawnes (see p. 54)	c. 1672–?
Mr Nicholas Archer (see p. 54)	c. 1672–?
Mr John Taylor (see p. 54)	c. 1672–?
Pastors in the first General Baptist Church	
Mr E. Kingsford (see p. 61)	1828–1829
Mr S. Wright (see p. 61)	1829–1852
Rev. John Crapps (see p. 62)	1852–1854
Pastors in the reconstituted General Baptist Church	
Rev. John Cookson (see p. 67)	1863–1873
Rev. E. Compton (see p. 69)	1973–1882
Student (name unknown) (see p. 71)	1882–1885
Pastors in Thomas Cooper Memorial Church, St Benedict's Square	
Rev. John E. Bennett (see p. 73)	1886–1894
Rev. Frederick A. Jackson (see p. 75)	1895–1901
Rev. Frank E. Miller (see p. 75)	1902–1908
Rev. R. T. Anderson (see p. 80)	1910–1912
Mr Claud M. Coltman (student) (see p. 81)	1912–1913
Rev. Charles H. Homer (see p. 81)	1914–1920

Pastors in Thomas Cooper Memorial Mission, St Benedict's Square
Rev. R. S. Bradbook (see p. 85)   1922–1923
Mr C. H. Radford (see p. 87)   1923–1924

Pastors in Thomas Cooper Memorial Church, St Benedict's Square
Mr C. H. Radford (see p. 89)   1924–1958
Rev. H. Whyte (see p. 93)   1959–1963
Rev. J. T. Orrell (see p. 94)   1966–1972

Pastors in Thomas Cooper Memorial Church, High Street
Rev. J. T. Orrell (see p. 94)   1972–1984
Rev. J. K. McClatchy (see p. 94)   1986–1994
Rev. R. Bedford (see p. 94)   1995–1999
Rev. Hugh Hill (see p. 95)   2000–2007
Rev. Mike Smailes (see p. 98)   2008–2013

Appendix 4

Miscellaneous articles and photographs

1. Order of Service – Laying of Foundation Stones, Thomas Cooper Memorial Church, St Benedict's Square, 6 April, 1885

Thomas Cooper Memorial Chapel,

ST. BENEDICT'S SQUARE, LINCOLN.

ON EASTER MONDAY, APRIL THE 6TH, 1885.

Order of the proceedings at the Ceremony of

LAYING ∴ MEMORIAL ∴ STONES

At 2 o'Clock p.m.

Hymn	....	No. 1.
Reading of Scripture	....	Rev. E. H. Jackson.
Prayer	....	Rev. J. Williamson, M.A.
Church Statement	....	The Pastor.
Hymn	....	No. 2.

The Stones will then be laid.

Doxology. Collection.

Brief Address by Various Ministers.

Hymn	....	No. 3.
Prayer	....	Rev. G. P. Mackay.

Adjournment to the Newland Congregational Church at 3.15.

Sermon by .... Dr. Clifford, M.A. LL.B., B.Sc.

Tea from 5 to 6 in the Newland Lecture Hall.

Evening at 7 o'Clock

A PUBLIC MEETING Will be held in the above Church. CHAIRMAN :—J. SMITH, ESQ. J.P.

Speakers:—Revs. W. ORTON, (Grimsby,) E. H. JACKSON, (Louth,) J. JOLLY, B.A. (Boston,)
J. WILLIAMSON, M.A., Dr. CLIFFORD, M.A., J. SAWTELL, E. METCALF, G. P. MACKAY,
R. CHEW, G. ANDERSON, *Pastor.*

A Collection will be made at each Service in aid of the Building Fund.

2. George Hood's Jubilee – special service, Tuesday, 18 April, 1911

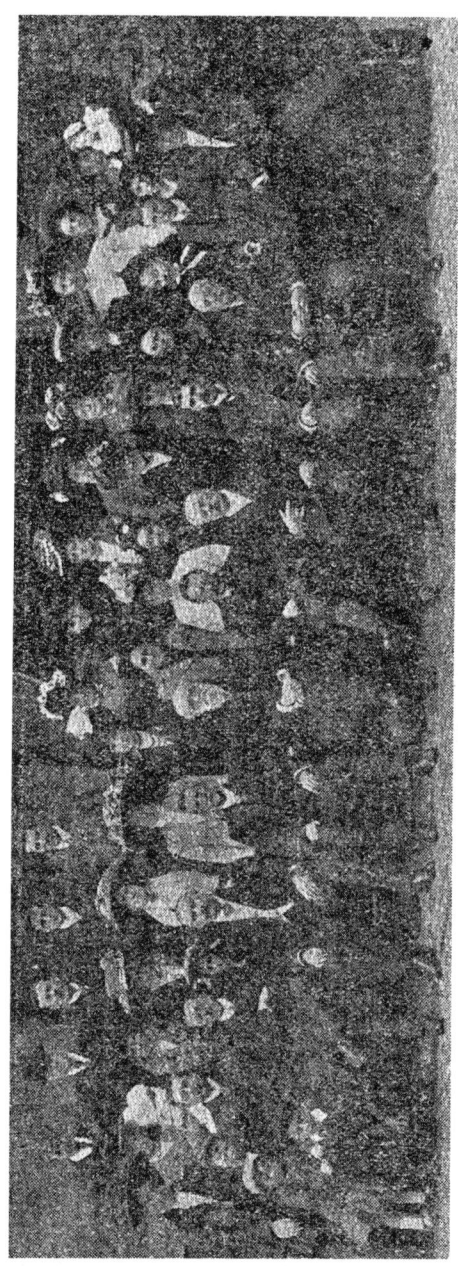

Lincoln Baptists and Dr Clifford

This excellent group will probably one day become historic. It was taken just before the special service, conducted by Dr Clifford on Tuesday afternoon. The names, reading from left to right are:

(*Top row*): J. Green, W. Walton, F. Smith, W. C. Hood, Mrs Cropper, Mrs Linton, Miss L. Colam, Miss Colam, Mrs Southern, Miss Yorke, Miss Neale, Miss Fountain

(*Second row*): Mrs Wilson, Mrs Lawson, Mrs Watson, Mrs Smith, Mrs G. F. Hood, Mrs Miller, Mrs Willerton, Mrs Bennet, Mrs Anderson, Mrs Jackson, Mrs Blake, Mrs J. Blake, Mrs Mawby, Mrs A. Muse, Mr C. Smith, Mrs Fountain, Mr Green

(*Bottom row – past and present officers*): Rev. F. E. Miller, Mr W. S. Linton, Mr H. Willerton, **Mr G. Hood**, Dr Clifford, Rev. R. T. Anderson (Pastor), Mr W. S. Oncken, Mr J. Blake, Mr T. W. Mawby

DR CLIFFORD IN LINCOLN
PRESENTATION TO MR. GEORGE HOOD

The Thomas Cooper Memorial Baptist Church, Lincoln, was crowded on Tuesday evening, on the occasion of the presentation of an illuminated address to Mr. George Hood, on the completion of fifty years' continuous membership of the church.

The Mayor (Mr. C. H. Newsum) was in the chair, being supported by the Rev. R. T. Anderson (Pastor), the Rev. G. Barrett, the Rev. F. E. Miller, the Rev. W. Walker, Mr. H. Willerton, Mr. F. S. Lambert, and Mr. W. S. Linton (Church Secretary).

The Mayor, in opening, referred to the object of the meeting, and said fifty years was a long time for a man to look back upon. Besides being Mr. Hood's jubilee, it was the jubilee of the Sunday School of the Church. It was impossible to grasp the possibilities of what that fifty years of work might mean for the good and welfare of the country at large. He spoke highly of the work of Mr. Hood, and said would that Lincoln had more men like him.

Dr. John Clifford then made the presentation with appropriate remarks, and later proceeded to address the meeting. He took as his subject the changes in religion in the last fifty years. One of the most important changes, he said, was the advance made by intrinsically spiritual religion. It was a change that had gone right to the life of the British people. It was not possible to made men with a hard logical mechanical basis for religion. There must be a union in heart – a union of intellectual sympathy. After dealing with several other changes, he went on to detail six points on what would happen during the next 50 years. He believed that religion would be brought more into municipal and political life, there would be finer application of Christian principles. Religion would completely christianise our lives. He did not believe in the decline of the churches. The social application would be more thorough and intensive. There would be greater personal independence and religious freedom. He went on to give some advice to the young people, and reminded them that they were the "hope of the future."

Then followed addresses by the Pastor, the Rev. F. E. Miller, and Rev. W. Walker.

Mr. Hood, in offering his thanks for the address, gave many deeply interesting reminiscences of his 50 years' connection with the Church.

(Reproduced from *Lincolnshire Echo*, Wednesday, 19 April, 1911)

3. Memorial Service for Dr Ian and Audrey Sharpe and family

(Reproduced from the *TCM Monthly Magazine*, February 1965)

On January 17th at our evening service, our Church was almost filled by a large congregation, who came to remember and give thanks for Dr Ian and Audrey Sharpe and their three children, Jillian Lynn (aged 8), Alison Joy (aged 7), and Andrew (aged 4). After a time of uncertainty and much prayer from many hearts, news was at last received, and later confirmed by the UFM [Unevangelized Fields Mission] Secretary, that Ian, Audrey and the children had been 'promoted to glory', as the Salvation Army aptly describe the experience men call death, which the Scriptures call 'falling asleep'.

Parents and friends of both Ian and Audrey were present at the service, and they were sustained in the trying experience.

Mr. C. H. Mason (Caravan Mission) was our guest preacher, and led the service, and he announced that the hymns had been chosen by Mrs. Allen (Audrey's mother). Each of the hymns were related to some aspect of the life of Ian, Audrey and the children. The hymns were, (1) *O Jesus, I have promised*, (2) *It may not be on the mountain's height*, (3) *The world looks very beautiful and full of joy to me*, (4) *Jesus shall reign where'er the sun*. The Choir ably rendered a request piece, *Onward still and upward*.

Mr. Mason offered prayer suitable to the occasion, and then read Romans 8:28–39, and there was great comfort as the words of certainty and triumph fell upon our ears, 'Who shall separate us from the love of Christ?' and 'Nothing shall be able to separate us from the love of God, which is in Christ Jesus our Lord'.

Mr. Bill Gilvear, who travelled from Glasgow to be present, said he would have 'come from the end of the world to pay tribute to Ian and Audrey', with whom he had worked in the

Dr Ian and Audrey Sharpe and their children – Jillian, Alison and Andrew. (Photos courtesy of Day One Publications)

Congo. He recalled how Ian continually used his surgical skill in difficult conditions, and that in spite of the many claims on his time, and tiring circumstances, Ian kept up to date in progressive medical knowledge. He said he loved Ian and Audrey for their dedication to their Lord, and their skill and patience in dealing with the sick and sorrowing. Audrey had a great way with children, and did a good work among the crowds that thronged the Mission Stations. Mr. Gilvear told of the frolics and games he played with young Andrew and his sisters, and though they are gone, the memory remains. Our brother gave us a helpful glimpse into the sphere and conditions where much faithful service was given until so suddenly cut short. Our brother's testimony must have been a help to all present.

Mr. V. A. West spoke on behalf of our Church, and said he found it very difficult to express the words that lay deep in our hearts, but above all the clanging voices that are in the world, and the sorrow in our own heart, we hear the voice of our glorified Lord, 'I am He that liveth and was dead and behold I am alive for ever more'. Though He is exalted in the unrevealed heavenly glory, yet His compassion and pity is unchanged. Our Church had a special interest in the work of God in the Congo, for Audrey was dedicated, baptised, married and went overseas from TCM, and when Ian came he entered our affection and interest, and we prayed for both. They responded to God's call and gladly went beyond the frontiers of civilisation, into the sphere of cruelty and superstition. They found that our Lord did not say 'Go to Africa' but 'Come to Africa' for He was there to meet them and use them. They went out equipped for their task, for they had learned the language, studied the tropical diseases they would have to deal with, and above all a passion to win souls for their Lord. They and we expected that their witness would be maintained for many years, or until our Lord's return, but in the mysterious will of God, this was not to be. We do not know details of the manner of their passing, but we know the Lord Jesus and are sure He was with them when the furnace was 'seven times heated' (Dan. 3:19).

Some tell us 'they *lost* their life', but they *gave* their life in their Lord's service, and this includes the children up to the measure of their understanding. Rev. 12:11 sums up their life; i.e. 'They overcame him by the blood of the Lamb, and by the word of their testimony, and they loved not their life unto the death'. The Saviour's sacrifice, their testimony and the final gift of life, and surely 'All the trumpets sounded for them on the other side'. Cynics sometimes say, 'Where was God when these things happened?', and many grief torn believers have had similar thoughts. A Minister was asked this question by a bereaved father, and after quiet prayer and thought replied, 'Just where He was when His own Son was on the cross in agony and shame'. God makes no mistakes, and He alone knows when our work is done. Men like Henry Martyn, David Brainard, Robert Murray McChene and many others went 'Home' young. 'He buries His workmen but carries on the work.' The prayerful sympathy of our Church was expressed to those who sorrow and will miss Ian, Audrey and the children most. Mr. Mason gave the concluding address, and recalled how Audrey had helped him in some of his missions, and her fruitful work among the children. He then made a passionate appeal to the young people to respond to the call of God, 'Whom shall I send and who will go for us?' (Isa. 6:8), and we believe that the appeal will not go unanswered.

(The above is only a summary of the service, for no words could reproduce the atmosphere of quiet rest and thanksgiving.)

Sympathy [from a former Pastor and his wife]: A letter has been received from the Rev. & Mrs. Harry Whyte expressing the prayerful sympathy of themselves and the City Road Baptist Church, Bristol, in the passing of Dr. Ian, Audrey and the children. They will continue to pray that God will comfort the sorrowing and join with us in looking for the return of our Lord Jesus Christ.

4. The move from St Benedict's Square

From The Pastor's Study
(A letter from the Pastor, Rev. R. T. Orrell, reproduced from the *TCM Monthly Magazine*, November 1967)

My dear Friend,

Following the Special Church Meeting, held on the 27th of September, this is the first opportunity I have had of writing about the very important matter which we discussed. News spreads rapidly, and most people who have an interest in our work will now be familiar with the decision which we took. It seems fitting, however, that I should devote this Pastoral Letter to assessing the situation.

A few years ago, Marks & Spencer Ltd, who have premises adjoining our own, approached the Church Trustees with a view to buying our Property. Nothing came of this, and the matter was thought to be closed. A few months ago, however, a further approach was made, this time direct from the Estate Department of Marks & Spencer in London. It was felt wise that the Trustees should meet a representative from the Company and accordingly, a meeting was held at the Manse on the 31st of August. In due course, the proposals put to the Trustees by Marks & Spencer were conveyed to the Special Church Meeting.

Those who were present at the Meeting were able to see a copy of the most recent plan, secured from the City Planning Office, showing intended developments for the city-centre area. The first stage of the plan is for an Inner Ring Road immediately at the back of our premises, with a bridge over the river. Even if this were the only development, it might well cause us concern. The work of constructing a road and bridge could considerably disturb the structure of our back premises, which are by far the older part of our property. But added to this, the thought of constant heavy traffic, with its vibration and noise, passing in such close proximity to the Church is not a welcome prospect. This, however, is not all. The plan also shows a Service Road, designed to cut right through the Schoolroom, across part of the Church Parlour, and swinging round alongside the Church – in the process of which it cuts off most of the Pastor's Vestry!

The property alongside us, now being used by the Lincoln-shire Echo as a garage, is, in actual fact, owned by Marks & Spencer, and they hope to take possession in about a year's time. Now, the lower part of this is also affected by the proposed new road. The approach of the Company to the Trustees, therefore, was along the lines of whether we could come to an agreement which would be to our mutual advantage. They would like to purchase our premises so as to build the intended extension of their Stores on the part not affected by City Development. In return for this, they will either:

1. Find us another city-centre site and build and equip for us a new Church and such other premises as we require for our work, or;
2. Make a sum of money available, so that the Church can secure its own site and be entirely responsible for erecting the buildings.

The choice was left with us and, in either case, the sum of money being offered is One Hundred Thousand Pounds.

We must not, of course, be tempted by merely material things. On the other hand, it is a serious responsibility to immediately refuse such an amount of money – serious because we have to prayerfully consider whether this may not well be a gracious provision of the Lord for us. Only today, the Minister of another Church, faced with a similar problem to our own, was 'phoning me about something. He had somehow heard about the offer made by Marks & Spencer to us, and expressed the wish that something similar could happen to his Church! Also, a Chartered Surveyor, with whom we have been in correspondence, says in one of his letters: 'What a wonderful opportunity.' Undoubtedly it is an important issue for us as a Church. What else can we desire but to know and do the Lord's will? It might help, therefore, if I set down a number of points to clarify our thoughts.

1. We are not unaware of the sentimental and even sacred associations which many have with the present building. Furthermore, all of us, no matter how long or short has been our link with TCM, must be aware that it is no light thing to uproot a work and seek to plant it elsewhere. As the Pastor involved at this time, I know that I feel a great sense of personal responsibility. We are not, however, unique in facing this situation. In many districts, the moving out of populations has made some places of worship become what we call 'down-town churches', often with dwindling congregations. Several of these have found it necessary to move out to more populous areas. Many others, like ourselves, are having to make some move because of town-centre redevelopment. In recent issues of the *Evangelical Times*, one cannot fail to notice the number of evangelical churches facing this same problem. But one is pleased to see how many, despite perhaps some sadness at leaving the old spiritual home, are facing it courageously and relying on the Lord's help. Even the famous Tent Hall in Glasgow is likely to disappear from its present situation, because a road is planned to go right through it!

2. We have not sought for this, but it may be significant that the approach has been made to us at a time when we have cause to be concerned about the future of our Church premises. Let us be quite clear that there is no attempt by Marks & Spencer to force us out and, in fact, they have been

most gracious and helpful in their approach. It is a well-known fact that they are an honourable firm, and I am sure that we have no need for anxiety in our dealings with them. They are, of course, Jews and the President of the Company, Lord Sieff, is a man with a great and active interest in the State of Israel – something which is also of interest to us!

3. Quite a number of people, with a very real spiritual concern for the Church – some in membership, but others who for many years have been close friends of TCM and live some distance away – have expressed the thought, after praying about the matter, that this thing is of the Lord. The confirmation of this will be the finding of a suitable city-centre site – for there is no question of our moving out of the city-centre area. I am not unaware of the difficulties there may seem to be in this matter, especially as others seem to have no success in finding land. But the Lord is on our side and if it is His will that we move, a suitable provision will be made. It could be to our advantage if, while remaining reasonably city-centre, we could be nearer some houses. Certainly, it might well help the Sunday School. We realise that, these days, there are many reasons for decreased Sunday School attendances, not only in Lincoln but also throughout the country. There is no doubt, however, that one problem for us is our complete detachment from any residential property.

4. As I have already written, we are not unaware of the close associations which many have with TCM, and some over many years. We must ever keep in mind, however, that the Church is not the *place* but the *people*. God's blessing is not on a building as such, but upon the faithful believers who worship and serve Him. It would be a great mistake to think that He cannot bless us somewhere else. It occurs to me that one of the best known missionary churches in the world – the People's Church in Toronto, where Dr Oswald Smith has

laboured for so many years – is now some considerable distance from where it used to be. But the work is still greatly blessed – people are constantly being saved there, missionaries sent out and every year [and] an increasing amount of money given for their support. God could do the same for us!

5. At present, a considerable amount of our weekly income has, of necessity, to be constantly spent on repairs and renewals of our present property. If we remain where we are, this spending on the building will have to continue, and with some of the things which require attention and the factor of rising costs, such spending will probably need to be increased. I fear that many who just move to and from meetings and never really have a good look around the building, are not aware of just all that does need attention. Even if the Church never had to move and reasonable repairs continued, there is bound to go on the general deterioration which one gets with property over passing years – especially a building as old as ours. But as we stay on and spend on it is always with the possibility that, one day, the property will have to come down. We know that Lincoln Corporation are notoriously slow and unreliable in carrying out proposed plans and, in fact, are constantly changing them. One cannot help but think, however, that the rate of traffic build-up in the city centre (an increasing factor with every year) will make it imperative that something be done. This is almost certain to involve the High Street and Brayford areas, and whatever the slowness in the past, may have to be done in the next few years.

6. Arising out of what I have just written is this further thought – if nothing happened to disturb the Church for 5, 10, 20, even 30 years, are we right in refusing such an offer and binding some future generation to the task of finding what could then be an even larger amount of money than is required now for new premises? Such accommodation as we require

could well cost around £70,000. What will this figure have become even in a few years' time? We can be sure of this – that if a Compulsory Purchase Order is made on the property in years to come, there is not likely to be the same cooperation in finding another city-centre site as there is now; and also, the amount of compensation would be totally inadequate.

All these things are challenging practical considerations, and as the Lord's people, we must be honest enough to face them. None of us knows what even tomorrow will bring. What then of the next few years? Many of us will no longer be here. Certainly, if we start thinking 20 or 30 years ahead we shall not be! Some will be living elsewhere, and not a few will have gone home to Glory. Indeed, the Lord may have come, and then buildings will not matter whether old or new! But we do not know the day nor the hour and we have to make our plans, always, of course, seeking the Lord's guidance. Let us therefore think of others who, in the future, may be called upon to carry on the work. If we can leave them the legacy of a new building, instead of having constantly to find money to repair an older property, they can do what many of us would like to be doing now – channelling our money more and more into direct spiritual work, such as the increased support of our missionaries and our own evangelistic efforts.

My main concern, as I write this, is that, whatever the final outcome, we should all be willing for God's will. Then, whether we stay or move, we cannot fail to know His blessing, both personally and as a Church. Can I ask that, difficult though it might be, we put aside all personal considerations and be concerned about the present and future spiritual prosperity of the work? This will need to be done sincerely. It is very easy to be self-deceived and to say: 'The Lord has blessed us here, and we shouldn't move', when we really mean that we do not want to!

If this does indeed prove to be a provision from the Lord, instead of being fearful and hesitant, let us thank Him, and rejoice in the privilege of having a share in what may be a further stage in the evangelistic witness of the Church. We are not foolish enough to think that a new building automatically makes crowds of people come rushing in. But a new start usually does mean new interest and contacts and attendances, and thus many more may hear the Gospel and be saved.

A very substantial majority at the Special Church Meeting agreed that we should negotiate further with Marks & Spencer. This we are now doing and when there is anything definite to report, the Church will be informed. In the meantime, I am going to ask for much prayer –

- That each one of us will be willing for His will.
- That He will show us His will very clearly.
- That knowing His will, we may carry it out with spiritual courage.
- That to those of us who have the responsibility of carrying out the negotiations, etc., wisdom will be given.
- That among all our Fellowship, there be a deepening of love, understanding, regard, and respect one for the other.
- That we might know in a fuller way the 'unity of the Spirit in the bond of peace' (Eph. 4:3).
- That even now God's manifest blessing will be on the work, with souls being saved, a deepening of the spiritual life of believers, and indeed such a working of the Holy Spirit in our midst that it might truly be termed revival.

The Lord bless and use you for His glory.

Your friend and Pastor,

J. T. Orrell

5. TCM officers (late 1940s – early 1950s)

[Back row]: Charlie Smith, Fred Scruton, Jack Wood, Tom Wood
[Front row]: Mr West, Cecil Radford (Pastor), Cyril Dean

6. Annie Bayram – missionary in Nigeria 1933–1961 with Sudan Interior Mission (SIM)

Annie Bayram's house in Paiko, Nigeria, constructed to her own design.
TCM sent £30 in 1935 to enable it to be built. The money was raised by
offering £1 shares, and share certificates issued (see below).

THOMAS COOPER MEMORIAL BUILDING SOCIETY.
St BENEDICTS SQUARE
— LINCOLN —
Nominal Capital £30 Divided into 7200 1ᴰ Shares

This is to Certify that Kath: Dawson & Percy blepham
is a registered holder of Twenty four Shares
of 1ᴰ Each - fully paid.

N.B. — This property is held by the Society
& is situated in PAIKO · NIGERIA WEST AFRICA.

Bibliography

Beale, D. (2000), *The Mayflower Pilgrims: Roots of Puritan, Presbyterian, Congregationalist, and Baptist Heritage*, Greenville, USA: Ambassador-Emerald International.

Conklin, R. J. (1935), *Thomas Cooper the Chartist (1805–1892)*, Manila: University of the Philippines Press.

Evans, B., *The Early English Baptists, Vol. 1*, Harvard University Library, http://baptisthistoryhomepage.com/1.google.books.links.html (accessed November 2014).

Hayes, M. (2002), *Missing, Believed Killed*, Surrey: Day One Publications.

Larsen, T. (ed.) (2003), *Biographical Dictionary of Evangelicals*, Leicester: Inter-Varsity Press.

Linton, W. S. (1911), *The History of the General Baptist Church in Lincoln*, Lincoln: TCM Library; Oxford: Angus Library, Regent's Park College.

Radford, C. H. (1948), *'These Five and Twenty Years': 1923–1948*, Lincoln: TCM Library.

Truby, D. W. (1966), *Congo Saga*, London: Unevangelized Fields Mission.

Underwood, A. C. (1947), *A History of the English Baptists*, London: The Baptist Union Publication Dept. (Kingsgate Press).

Whitley, W. T., *Minutes of the General Assembly of the General Baptist Churches in England*, Cornell University Library, http://archive.org/stream/cu31924092446297/cu31924092446297_djvu.txt (accessed November 2014).